portland 4th edition

eat

00 about
01 author notes
02 maps
104 twenty favorites
105 hotels

acme 03
alberta street 05
oyster bar & grill
alma chocolate 07
annie's donut shop 09
autentica 11
bakery bar 13
binh minh bakery & deli 15
blue moose cafe 17
bumblekiss 19
café castagna 21
castagna 23
ciao vito 25
clarklewis 27
cork 29
crema 31
curds & whey 33
fat city cafe 35
foxfire teas 37
good taste restaurant 39
ken's artisan pizza 41
le pigeon 43
navarre 45
nostrana 47
pacific supermarket 49
park kitchen 51
pastaworks 53
pix pâtisserie 55
pok pok 57
ristretto roasters 59
roux 61
sahagun 63
saint cupcake 65
saucebox 67
savoy tavern and bistro 69
simpatica dining hall 71
sohbet 73
sweets etc. 75
sydney's 77
tabor 79
the busy corner 81
the florida room 83
valentine's 85
vindalho 87
wildwood 89

107 bedford brown
109 bella flora studio
111 black wagon
113 bolt
115 canoe
117 cargo
119 cheeky b
121 close knit
123 denwave
125 ed's house of gems
127 flutter
129 foundation garments
131 fuchsia
133 gr scrub
135 hello portland
137 hive
139 imp
141 indigo traders
143 ivy studio
145 lark press
147 le train bleu
149 mabel and zora
151 mimi & lena
153 missing link
155 moshi moshi
157 moxie
159 muse art & design
161 oblation papers & press
163 odessa
165 office
167 opal
169 phlox
171 polliwog
173 portland modern
175 possession
177 quinn in the city
179 shag
181 souchi
183 space design
185 switch shoes
187 the lippman company
189 una
191 yes

S0-BCA-142

acme

good food, good drink

1305 se 8th street. corner of main
503.230.9020 www.acme-pdx.com
daily 4p - after midnight

opened in 2005. owners: kevin dorney and marcus goomba
owner / chef: jon beeaker
$: all major credit cards accepted
dinner. late night. full bar. live music. first come, first served

southeast : industrial district > **e1**

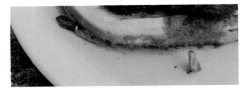

there's nothing worse than getting together with friends trying to figure out where to go to dinner. it often feels like a parliamentary procedure with the lefties voting brew and grub and the righties voting mixed drinks and cuisine. to those factions who just can't work it out, i have the answer: *acme* -—it's got it all for the bicker-sons: great beer, a plethora of classic cocktails and pub fare that raises the genre to a whole new level. burgers are made from bison, and the ribs are wild boar. and just in case you feel the need for some korean snacks, there's freshly made kimchee. *acme's* an original.

imbibe:
the el presidente
mint julep

devour:
grilled quail rubbed with a sweet chile jam
the east side jumble salad
wild boar ribs
acme's house-smoked pulled pork & slaw
bread puddin'

alberta street oyster bar & grill

a neighborhood restaurant featuring the foods of the pacific northwest

2926 ne alberta street. between 29th and 30th
503.284.9600 www.albertaoyster.com
mon, wed - sun 4:30p - close

opened in 2005. owner: peter hochman   chef: eric bechard
$$: all major credit cards accepted
dinner. full bar. happy hour. reservations recommended

northeast : alberta > **e2**

i grew up in southwest portland in the '70s when there was no such thing as a neighborhood restaurant, at least not in my neck of the woods. today the city is filled with these fantastic restaurants. one that has been embraced from the moment it opened is *alberta street oyster bar & grill*. peter rolled out the welcome mat to the 'hood, and soon after scads of happy albertians were spreading the word that *alberta street* was hitting just the right spot—upscale, but not fancy—beautifully prepared food, but not fussy. love at first bite.

imbibe:
the classic martini
bloody mary oyster shooter

devour:
oysters on the half shell (duh)
salmon tartare with sturgeon caviar
smoked duck salad with peaches &
   goat cheese
deconstructed rootbeer float

alma chocolate

housemade chocolates using fair trade and organic ingredients

140 ne 28th avenue. corner of davis
503.517.0262 www.almachocolate.com
tue - sat 11a - 6p

opened in 2006. owner: sarah hart
$: mc. visa
treats. first come, first served

northeast : 28th > **e3**

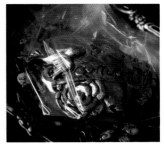

portlanders are very supportive of the arts. each month there are first and last thursday events that attract throngs of people who come to look at and discuss art, and yes... drink lots of wine. but i suggest to the art connoisseurs that they should expand their horizons beyond the galleries and check out the edible art at *alma chocolate*. sarah is molding her carefully chosen chocolate into religious icons and mexican style milagros that if you don't immediately eat (and you will) or give as a special gift, would look pretty spectacular hanging on a wall.

devour:
chocolate icons
habañero crowns
ginger almond toffee
lime & piñon barks
bourbon bonbons
the colette
smoked paprika truffles

annie's donut shop

fresh donuts

3449 ne 72nd avenue. intersection of fremont and sandy
503.284.2752
daily 5a - 10pm sat 5a - 5p

$: mc. visa
treats. first come, first served

northeast : rose city > **e4**

in the mid '90s i bought a house on northeast 72nd avenue. i loved this house, but what i really loved was that it was only three blocks away from *annie's donut shop*. i soon had my *annie's* schedule: mondays were for old fashioneds, wednesdays called for cinnamon twists and weekends and special occasions i saved for the king of donuts: the bismark. *annie's* may be a bit off the beaten path, but honestly—wouldn't you travel just about anywhere to get a really good donut? sure you would.

imbibe:
cold milk
hot coffee

devour:
maple old-fashioneds
devil's food donuts
cinnamon twists
cream cheese flips
buttermilk bars

autentica

authentic mexican cuisine

3507 ne 30th avenue. corner of killingsworth
503.287.7555
tue - fri 11a - 10p sat - sun 10a - 3p and 5 - 10p

opened in 2006. owners: oswaldo bibiano and evelia madrano
$$: all major credit cards accepted
lunch. dinner. brunch. full bar. first come, first served

northeast : killingsworth > **e5**

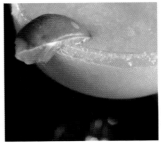

any menu that has queso on it is a good menu. i love the stuff so much that i dedicated an entire *eat.shop guide* to it (austin). and though my very favorite queso is the variety my austin pal marianne whips up: melted velveeta with spicy rotelle (canned tomatoes, onions and peppers) mixed in, i know that this is an aberration. if you want the real thing, which i will admit to being hugely (this is the size you will be if you eat too much) satisfying, head to *autentica*. their queso is oozing with cheesy goodness and is studded with chewy chunks of chorizo. take that velveeta.

imbibe:
house sangria
jarritos

devour:
tamales de pollo chiles poblano y crema agria
queso oaxaco con chorizo servido con
   tortillas de maiz o harina
carne a la plancha con frijoles charros y
   chiles toreados

bakery bar

custom cake and dessert studio

1028 se water avenue. corner of taylor
503.546.8110 www.bakerybar.com
mon - fri 7:30a - 6p sat 8a - 3p

opened in 2005. owner and chef: jocelyn barda
$: mc. visa
breakfast. lunch. treats. first come, first served

southeast : industrial district > **e6**

this is the fourth edition of *eat.shop.portland* and for those of you who have them all, you know this: i. love. baked. goods. in this edition alone i am featuring six different bakery / pâtisserie meccas and i could have done more—it's pure trauma to decide where to go. when i'm traumatized, *bakery bar* relieves the anguish. jocelyn is creating sweet beauties ranging from exquisite wedding cakes (italian orange olive oil cake! banana bourbon cake!) to homemade ice cream sandwiches. there are soooo many good things, that new trauma is induced when deciding what to get. sigh.

imbibe:
the forklift (house coffee & espresso shot)
lucky lab ipa

devour:
coconut cream puffs
earl grey tea shortbreads
sharp cheddar scallion bacon scones
egg salad sandwiches
custom wedding & birthday cakes

13

binh minh bakery & deli

vietnamese sandwiches, breads and pastries

6812 ne broadway. corner of 68th
503.257.3868
mon - thu 9a - 6p fri - sun 8a - 5p

opened in 2002. owner: van le
$: cash
breakfast. lunch. first come, first served

northeast : rose city > **e7**

my *binh minh bakery & deli* story goes like this. i called my pal chris (chef at *saucebox*) and i said, "let's go to the vietnamese sandwich place that you and andy (chef/owner of *pok pok*) like." an hour later we were sitting at one of the two tables at *binh minh* devouring vietnamese sandwiches, which we discovered are radically good when dipped into the divine beef stew. it was a race to see who could sop up the last drip of stew. i broke concentration for a mere second to sip my lychee drink and chris swooped in. never trust chefs; they're highly-trained eating machines.

imbibe:
foco lychee drink
chin chin grass jelly drink vietnamese coffee

devour:
vietnamese sandwich
meatball sandwich
vietnamese noodles with pork
beef stew with french bread
colorful desserts

blue moose cafe

wholesome vegetarian food
4936 ne fremont. corner of 49th
503.548.4475
daily 9a - 8p

opened in 2005. owner: sheila gilronan
$: mc. visa
breakfast. lunch. dinner. beer and wine. first come, first served

northeast : beaumont village >

when dog's dig deli closed down a couple of years back, i cried. you would have sobbed too if you had eaten sheila's warm chocolate chip cookies. but take heart! sheila has opened *blue moose cafe* and being the lovely woman that she is, she chose a location just blocks away from my house. *blue moose* is the perfect pdx neighborhood spot with its homey interior and great little patio. the menu is bursting with vegetarian goodness of which even non-veggies like myself drool over. and yes, my tears have dried because the cookies are on the menu. praise be to the cookie gods.

imbibe:
blueberry ice tea
nikolina (croatian double espresso with
    whipped cream)

devour:
squirrel's feast
grilled peanut butter & banana sandwich
children of the corn sacrifice popeye
the best chocolate chip cookies ever

bumblekiss

eclectic comfort food

3517 ne 46th avenue. corner of fremont
503.282.6313 www.bumblekissrestaurant.com
tue - fri 7:30a - 2:30p sat - sun 8am - 3pm

opened in 2006. owners: lisa and vincent chavez chefs: rené sosa and clay card
$: mc. visa
breakfast. lunch. first come, first served

northeast : beaumont village > **e9**

one day as i'm hanging outside of my house, my neighbor bart ambles over for a chat. soon he's telling me about *bumblekiss*—did he say rumblefish? the toothless bumble from *rudolph*? huh? in my confusion, i blanked on his recommendation until sometime later when i was pulling a u-turn on fremont and noticed a brilliant orange little structure. reverse u-turn and there i was in front of *bumblekiss* which may be the cutest darn café ever. lickety-split i was in the door and soon i was swooning over the menu where everything is guaranteed to whet your whistle. thank you, bart.

imbibe:
organic coffee

devour:
burly benny
cinnamon swirl french toast
kids green eggs 'n' ham
scrumdillyumptious sandwich
le monstre
strawberries & melted chocolate for dipping

café castagna

modern bistro

1758 se hawthorne blvd. corner of poplar
503.231.9959 www.castagnarestaurant.com
daily 5:30p - close

opened in 2000. owners: kevin gibson and monique siu   chef: kevin gibson
$$: all major credit cards accepted
dinner. full bar. reservations for five or more

café castagna is the only restaurant in portland that has a fairy garden. i shouldn't be telling you this because my five-year-old daughter lola will be grumpy that i'm sharing insider information. but if you were ever wondering why people looked so blissed-out dining al fresco at *café castagna,* it's because there are fairies that are living in the lush landscaping of lavender and mint and fennel and cardoons—and they are sprinkling fairy dust in the form of dungeness crab salad, blood orange sorbet and tart cherry fizz cocktails. lola says there's magic here, and i'm a believer.

imbibe:
the miss scarlett
the karlovy tea

devour:
linguine with cockles, garlic & chili flake
roast chicken with walnut butter & sunchoke
pyrenees lamb meatballs with zolfino beans
duck fat brussels sprouts & turnips
gelato affogato

castagna

modern european cuisine

1752 se hawthorne blvd. corner of poplar
503.231.7373 www.castagnarestaurant.com
wed - sat 5:30p - close

opened in 1999. owners: kevin gibson and monique siu   chef: kevin gibson
$$ - $$$: all major credit cards accepted
dinner. full bar. reservations recommended

southeast : ladd's addition > **e11**

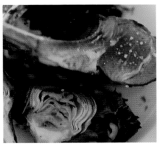

recently kevin (my husband) and i went to *café castagna* to have our weekly date. we propped ourselves up at the bar and asked to see the menu from *castagna* next door. suddenly a light went on in our addled brains and we realized instead of fantasizing about *castagna's* menu, we should just pick our lazy selves up and take the ten steps to eat there. soon we were sitting in the cozy back booth sipping david's perfect too-the-brim martinis and diving into a plate of kevin's house-cured lomo and we were, in a word, happy.

imbibe:

larmandier-bernier, vertus, blanc de blancs, brut
puffenay, "les bérangères" trousseau,arbois 2002

devour:
goose breast prosciutto, artichoke heart &
  mâche salad
gnocchi all romana
roast rack of lamb with pike's peak squash gratin
mascarpone cheesecake with seasonal berries

ciao vito

rustic italian

2203 ne alberta street. between 22nd and 23rd
503.282.5522 www.ciaovito.net
mon - thu 5 - 10p fri - sat 5 - 10:30p sun 5 - 10p

opened in 2004. owner / chef: vito dilullo
$$: mc. visa
dinner. reservations recommended

northeast : alberta > e12

here's my routine at *ciao vito*. i walk in and head to the counter that fronts the kitchen. i say, "hey, vito" and vito says "hey, kaie." then i say, "what's good, vito" and then he swings into action. in moments, a just-out-of-the-oven cobbler is presented, emitting the most wicked aroma of berries and stone fruits. i get a bit weak-kneed, but i'm not that easy, so i give the international sign for show me more. soon there are dishes lined up that all look luscious, and my urge is to grab them and run into a dark corner and gorge. but i catch hold of my dignified self and just say "hey, vito, it all looks good."

imbibe:
the sanguinante ceppo
selvapiana chianti rufina

devour:
crispy housemade meatballs with
  mozzarella & salsa rossa
linguini with butter poached dungeness crab
camp fire napolean of cinnamon phyllo,
  milk chocolate mousse & marshmallow

clarklewis

inventive seasonal italian

1001 se water avenue. corner of taylor
503.235.2294 www.clarklewispdx.com
mon - sat 5:30p - close

opened in 2004. owners: naomi pomeroy and morgan brownlow.
chef: morgan brownlow
$$: all major credit cards accepted
dinner. full bar. reservations recommended

southeast : industrial district > **e13**

so who knew that little old portland could be such a hotbed of rumours? but this past summer when the dynamic folks behind the *ripe* triangle of *family supper*, *gotham tavern* and *clarklewis* announced that the first two businesses would shutter, the pdx foodies went a bit berserk with tall tales. so i'm here now to get on the bandwagon and start a new rumour—*clarklewis* has beautiful food. yep, there it is. morgan uses carefully sourced, interesting ingredients that he transforms into simple, gorgeous cuisine. look no further for the truth because it's in the food.

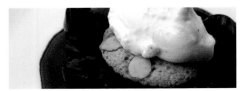

imbibe:
strawberry martini with basil & aged balsamic
bitter artichoke on the rocks

devour:
shaved speck ham wrapped around apricots
  with spring hill farm frisée & goat cheese
tagliatelle with guanciale &
  fried walla walla onions
warm peach & bing cherry streusel crostada

cork

a bottle shop

2901 ne alberta street. corner of 29th
503.281.cork www.corkwineshop.com
wed - sat 11a - 7p sun noon - 5p

opened in 20006. owner: darryl joannides
$ - $$: all major credit cards accepted
wine tasting dinners. classes. cork club. online shopping. delivery

northeast : alberta > **e14**

i'm going to be bold and i may offend some, but here it goes: *two buck chuck* is nasty wine. people, don't drink wine that costs the same amount as a bag of fried pork rinds. so you don't have a big budget—who does? the good news is that there are some amazing wines available that don't cost much more than your *'chuck.* don't believe me? head to *cork.* darryl has made it easy for you—a good chunk of this cool shop is under 20 dollars. you'll feel so flush with cash, not only will you buy good wine, but also chocolate, some bulk olive oil, and you'll want to sign up for a wine-tasting dinner.

imbibe:
2004 kaiken malbec (argentina)
2004 cascina castle't barbera d'asti (italy)
2004 jk carriere "provocateur" pinot noir (oregon)
2003 maison d'aupilhac cocaléres rouge (france)

devour:
extra virgin olive oil in bulk
charles chocolates caramelized rice krispies

crema

coffee and bakery
2728 se ankeny. corner of 28th
503.234.0206 www.cremabakery.com
mon - sat 7a - 6p sun 7:30a - 5p

opened in 2004. owner: brent fortune
$: mc. visa
breakfast. lunch. treats. first come, first served

southeast : 28th > **e15**

so as you know, i love bakeries. but for a while, i resisted *crema*. what got into me, you ask? a serious wheat allergy? bloating from too many cinnamon rolls? nope, i was a fan of the previous bakery *florio* that inhabited the *crema* space and i questioned whether *crema* would be as satisfying, so i stayed clear. *stupido*. though *florio* was pretty great, *crema* is really great. in fact i would say that denying myself the manchego and mushroom savory biscuits would fall in the "kaie is a knucklehead" category. but i have learned my lesson, and forever more my allegiance is with *crema*.

---

imbibe:
spanish latte
ginger lemonade

devour:
orange ginger scone
manchego mushroom savory biscuit
chocolate sable cookie
coconut creme cake
tuna dill sandwich on housemade ciabatta roll

curds & whey

purveyors of fine cheese and other essentials

8036 se 13th avenue. corner of spokane
503.231.2877 www.pdxcheese.com
tue - sat 11a - 7p sun noon - 5p

opened in 2005. owners: david schiffelbein and colin irwin
$$: all major credit cards accepted
lunch. grocery. first come, first served

southeast : sellwood > e16

when kevin and i travel, instead of visiting museums and tourist spectacles, we head for wet markets and food shops. the places that attract us are the ones that feel as though there's history behind them, as though there's a patina of authenticity. when i walked into *curds & whey*, i got this hit. though they have only been in business a year, david and colin wisely located their charming cheese store and café in a 1908 sellwood house which at one point housed a butcher shop. there's a little bit of lots of good things here: artisanal cheeses, wines, oils and other delicious sundries. yum.

imbibe:
2004 j.christopher zoot allure rouge
villa vella organic lemonade

devour:
five-year-old gouda from holland
great hill blue cheese
the café's cheese plate
le pere pelletier fisherman salt
wood cheese service boards from vermont

fat city cafe

classic portland diner

7820 sw capitol highway. between 35th and 36th
503.245.5457
daily 6:30a - 3p

opened: over 30 years ago owners: mark and helen johnson $: cash
breakfast. lunch. first come, first served

southwest : multnomah village > **e17**

flashback. 1982. wilson high school. it's 5th mod (is there still the mod system anywhere?) and i'm heading to *fat city* with my pals stephanie and mary. we pile into my half-vinyl honda and within minutes we're sitting at our regula' booth, ordering coffee, cinnamon rolls and grilled ham & cheeses. we're seventeen, so even though we say we're on a diet, that just means we pass on the milkshakes. *fat city* was cool then, and it's cool now. this is a portland landmark and i'm telling you, don't go there and try to stay on a diet. the chili-cheese-onion-fries on a foot-long will mock you.

imbibe:
the real deal milkshakes
good coffee

devour:
chicken-fried steak
grilled ham & cheese
chili dog
spam & eggs
cinnamon roll

foxfire teas

modern tea bar

4605 ne fremont street. corner of 46th avenue
503.288.6869 www.foxfireteas.com
see website for seasonal hours

opened in 2004. owners: quinn and katherine losselyong
$: all major credit cards accepted
breakfast. lunch. light dinner. beer and wine. first come, first served

northeast : fremont > **e18**

i was in boston earlier this year and while i was there i stopped by a local tea emporium. i checked out the menu and saw that they had matcha, so i ordered a latte. the guy behind the counter looked at me like i was a freaky, west coast tea dilettante. he was right—but before long i convinced him to make me one. tragedy. i should have known better than to try to re-create any of *foxfire tea's* fine drinks. quinn and katherine have the golden touch and not just with tea, but also with scones, sandwiches, salads and creating a rockin' good scene at night when wine and beer flow in place of tea.

imbibe:
matcha iced latte
jasmine basket tea

devour:
egg, ham & cheese breakfast sandwich
greek salad
nuvrei macaroons

covet:
eva solo tea brewer

good taste restaurant

chinese bbq and noodles

18 nw 4th avenue. corner of burnside
503.223.3838
daily 10a - 8p

opened in 1994. owner: shang chen
$: all major credit cards accepted
breakfast. lunch. dinner. first come, first served

northwest : old town > **e19**

there's a part of me that really wants to be a vegetarian. when i put faces on meals, i can lose my appetite pretty quickly. but when i think i might put meat on the back burner for good, i remember two things: bacon and roasted duck. i can say positively that there's not a soy product on the face of this earth that can compete with a slice of crispy duck. one of the best places in town to fulfill your carnivorous fowl (and pig) urges is *good taste*. the combination of the duck and egg noodles is heaven and will have you and your eating mates battling for the last crispy bits.

imbibe:
hot tea
soy bean drink

devour:
roasted duck with egg noodles
wonton noodle soup
oon choy with black bean sauce
scrambled eggs with bbq pork over rice
bbq spareribs

ken's artisan pizza

wood-fired pizzas

304 se 28th avenue. corner of pine
503.517.9951 www.kensartisan.com
tue - thu 5 - 9:30p fri - sat 5 - 11p

opened in 2006. owner: ken forkish   chef: alan maniscalco
$$: all major credit cards accepted
dinner. reservations accepted for eight or more

28th and burnside > **e20**

when i walked into *ken's artisan pizza* for the first time, i was in heaven. you might immediately assume it was because i caught a whiff of the pizza, but no, you would be wrong. it was the smell of the wood-burning oven that had me head-over-heels and reminding me of late fall when the crisp air at dusk smells of wood fires crackling in fireplaces. ummm... magic. the oven here is smack in the middle of the room which makes pizza the central focus, as it should be, because here it's simply divine. there are only a few to choose from, so loosen up the waistband and try them all.

imbibe:
bittburger pils
2005 cameroni giovanni

devour:
caesar salad
roasted veggie plate
margherita & arugula pizza
fennel sausage & roasted onion pizza
roasted apricots with pistachios & mascarpone

le pigeon

funky, sexy bistro

738 e burnside. corner of 8th
503.546.8796
wed - sun 5 - 11p brunch sat - sun 9am - 3pm

opened in 2006. owner: paul brady chef: gabriel rucker
$$: all major credit cards accepted
dinner. brunch. wine and beer. reservations for four or more

northeast : lower burnside > e21

squab, also known by the lowbrow name of pigeon, is one of my favorite foods. when i lived in los angeles, my ulimate restaurant, *campanile*, served it, and i still dream of that meal. so when i saw that *colleen's* had become *le pigeon*, i knew that whoever was behind the new name was barking up the right tree. soon after, i found myself perched at *le pigeon's* counter with the new chef gabe, yapping away like old pals. the moment he put a bone marrow sandwich with parsley salad in front of me he went straight to friends-forever status. gabe's a star and his food is outta this world.

imbibe:
04 "the wolf trap" boekenhoutskloof
st. peter's english ale

devour:
bone marrow & caramelized onion sandwich
radishes & spring peas with a broken butter &
   moscatel vinaigrette
strawberry mountain burger on a ciabatta bun
chocolate sea salt tart with mint pesto

navarre

small plates, great glasses
10 ne 28th avenue. corner of burnside
503.232.3555 www.eatnavarre.com
sun - thu 8a - 4p and 5:30 - 10:30p fri - sat 8a - 4p and 5:30 - 11:30p

opened in 2002. owners: john taboada and susan chaney chef: john taboada
$$: mc. visa
breakfast. lunch. dinner. first come, first served

northeast : 28th avenue > **e22**

i walk into *navarre* and john asks me if i want to get a picture of mushrooms. as always, i say yes and get myself in position to take a shot of one of john's spot-on delicious creations. he picks up a huge bucket and dumps about twenty pounds of gorgeous sliced porcini on the bar counter. he noted there was thirty pounds more, but i stopped him before the great *navarre* porcini pile overtook the whole restaurant. though *navarre* is famous for their small plates, john does things in a big way. big flavors, big glasses of wine, big happy full bellies.

imbibe:
2005 cameron giuliano box white table wine
2003 casamaro tinto rueda

devour:
john's famous pickle plate
seabeans, porcini & chard stems
salmon with corona beans
lamb plate: lamb chop, lamb sausage & lamb ham
basque cake

nostrana

playing with fire nightly

1401 se morrison. corner of 15th
503.234.2427 www.nostrana.com
lunch mon - fri 11a - 2p dinner sun - thu 5 - 10p fri - sat 5 - 11p

opened in 2005. owners: cathy whims, david west, marc and deb accuardi
chefs: cathy whims and deb accuardi
$$: all major credit cards accepted
lunch. dinner. reservations accepted for parties of six or more

southeast : industrial district >

nostrana has had a big year. within days of opening last fall, word spread that the pizza coming out of the wood-fire oven was gooood, and the lines started forming. not long after, it was named the restaurant of the year by the *oregonian* and there was nobody in portland who didn't know about *nostrana*. but beyond all the accolades, here beats the heart of a restaurant that's not about the hype but is about making food that appeals to everyone from 3 to 90 year olds. yes, the pizzas are delicious, but don't pass up the silky pastas and savory rotisserie chicken or you'll be sorry.

imbibe:
italian lemonade
1999 renato ratti barolo "conca"

devour:
antipasti misti
pollo arrosto from the rotisserie
sofia pizze
housemade fettucine with peas & fava beans
wood oven nectarine & purple raspberry crisp

pacific supermarket

asian market

6750 ne broadway street. corner of 67th
503.251.0524
daily 9am - 7pm

opened in 1997. owner: thu pham
$: all major credit cards accepted
groceries

**northeast : rose city > **

when i was next door having lunch at *binh minh bakery & deli*, i had my eye on *pacific supermarket*. kevin and i shop at *uwajimaya* and *fubonn*, which are both well-known asian supermarkets, but i had never gone into *pacific*. i knew i'd hit the jackpot when i saw the huge buddha at the entrance. though this market is not as vast or swanky as the other two, it carries a really intriguing mix of products. though i get seduced by the brightly colored packaging with cool graphics, my basket was mainly loaded with fresh lychees and ramens which are staples in our household.

imbibe:
great tea selection

devour:
stir-fried kimchee ramen
mandisa juicy chews
fresh lychees
sweet & sour lotus rootlet
fresh meats & fish
interesting selection of to-go foods

park kitchen

modern tavern cuisine

422 nw 8th avenue. between flanders and glisan
503.223.7275 www.parkkitchen.com
lunch mon - fri 11:30a - 2p dinner mon - sat 5p - close

opened in 2003. owner/chef: scott dolich
$$: mc. visa
lunch. dinner. full bar. reservations recommended

northwest : pearl district >

for father's day, i took my parents and kevin and lola to dinner at *park kitchen* and held my breath. i had no worries with kevin and my mother as they'll eat anything, but my dad and lola can be wild cards when it comes to their food likes/dislikes. to be safe, i ordered the chef's tasting menu with its wide variety of dishes (safety in numbers). after the plates began arriving, my father had a big "i like this food" grin on his face and lola was hogging whole plates to herself. bingo! it only got ugly when i went in for a bite of the chocolate campfire sundae and lola started growling...

imbibe:
the alamagoozlum
lost coast downtown brown beer

devour:
the chef's tasting menu
chickpea fries with pumpkin ketchup
sliced duck breast, hominy & english peas
roman style gnocchi, porcini & asparagus
chocolate campfire sundae

pastaworks

fresh pasta, artisan cheeses and good wine

se: 3735 se hawthorne blvd. between 37th and 38th. 503.232.1010
city market: 735 nw 21st avenue. corner of johnson. 503.221.3002
www.pastaworks.com
mon - sat 9:30a - 7p sun 10a - 7p

opened in 1983. owners: the de garmo family
$$: all major credit cards accepted
grocery

southeast : hawthorne / northwest : nob hill >

House Made
Pancetta

$11.99 lb

disclaimer! warning! *pastaworks* is not only owned by my husband's family but it may also be dangerous to your health. if you eat their handmade ravioli and fresh-baked focaccia with a big glass of chilled italian rosé you will feel unreasonably happy and you will be tempted to throw caution to the wind and eat carbs (oh my!) more than once a year. i faced up to the danger when i married kevin five years ago and folks, i'm still here. in fact, i'd go so far to say that whenever kevin makes me a carbonara with *pastaworks's* housemade pancetta, i'm the most satisfied woman alive.

imbibe:
hot lips strawberry soda
campagnol costieres de nimes rose box wine

devour:
handmade dungeness crab ravioli
fresh tuscan sheep's milk ricotta
housemade pancetta
strianese brand natural canned tomatoes
theo's 3400 phinney chocolate factory bars

pix pâtisserie

whimsical pastries, chocolates and savories

north: 3901 n williams. corner of failing. 503.282.6539
sun - thu 7am - midnight fri - sat 7am - 2am
southeast: 3402 se division. corner of 34th. 503.232.4407
sun - thu 10am - midnight fri - sat 10am - 2am
www.pixpatisserie.com

opened in 2003. owner: cheryl wakerhauser
$: all major credit cards accepted
breakfast. lunch. dinner. full bar. treats. events. first come, first served

north : nopo / southeast : division >

some portlanders tell me that because they live on the westside, they don't like to drive to the eastside because it takes too long or vice versa. my eyes start a-rollin' with this explanation because this is portland where you can be halfway to the beach in 30 minutes. but last year when *pix pâtisserie* opened on north williams i did a little jig because it was closer to my home than the other location in southeast. ah ha! can you say hyp-o-crite? i take back all eye-rolls—but am still giddy that the delightful world of pix and its shazams, jane avrils and jewel-like chocolates are just minutes away.

imbibe:
café carretto
french 75

devour:
salmon rillettes with cucumber salad
pig in a blanket
croquembouche
shazam!
marggie lane's potluck pleaser

pok pok

thai roasted chicken

3226 se division. between 32nd and 33rd
503.232.1387
mon - sat lunch 11:30a - 3:30p dinner 4:30- 9p

opened in 2005. owner: andy ricker
$: mc. visa
lunch. dinner. full bar. first come, first served

southeast : division >

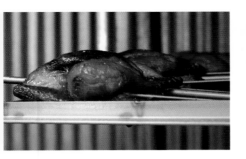

this past winter i had a food obsession. i woke up in the morning dreaming of khao soi kai, the chicken curry noodle soup at *pok pok*. the obsession grew in my head (and stomach) and i would imagine that every time i ate it that it: made me taller, smarter, nicer and younger. in my mind, this food could right all wrongs and i began to believe that every argument in this world would end if people would just sit down and eat khao soi kai. andy, to save humanity, you must spread the khao soi kai—you are our only hope obi-wan andy.

imbibe:
young coconut juice
cha manao: thai iced tea with fresh lime juice

devour:
khao soi kai (chiang mai style noodle soup)
pok pok special: 1/2 roasted game hen with
  green papaya salad
khao man som tam (shredded pork on
  coconut rice)

ristretto roasters

hand-crafted coffee

3520 ne 42nd avenue. corner of fremont
503.284.6767 www.ristrettoroasters.com
mon - fri 6:30a - 6p sat 7a - 6p sun 7a - 5p

opened in 2005. owner: din johnson
$: mc. visa
coffee. treats. online shopping. first come, first served

northeast : beaumont village > **e29**

i like my neighborhood. though nobody would consider beaumont village the epicenter of hipness, it does have one of the coolest little coffee joints in town: *ristretto roasters*. if you're a coffeehead, then i know you've made a beeline to *ristretto* because very quickly din made himself a stellar reputation with his roasting abilities. from tanzanian peaberry to ethiopian harrar beans, he's sourcing the good stuff. and to complement these fine coffees, his other half nancy is baking up some mighty fine baked goods. can you say pound (and a half, for good measure) cake? yes, please.

imbibe:
beautiful espresso
con panna
kid's hot chocolate

devour:
pound and a half cake
nancy's chocolate chip cookies
the eccles bar
pecan balls

roux

modern-style, classic french creole cuisine

1700 n killingsworth street. corner of concord
503.285.1300 www.rouxrestaurant.us
mon - thu 5 - 10p fri - sat 5 - 11p sun 5 - 9p brunch 10a - 2p

opened in 2005. owners: dwayne beliakoff and t.j. mchugh   chef: josh blythe
$$: all major credit cards accepted
dinner . brunch. full bar. happy hour. reservations recommended

north : nopo > **e30**

i've been to dinner at *roux* a number of times and each time, i'm a happy girl. somewhere between the obituary cocktail and the crawfish pie a smile becomes plastered on my face, and i just get all southern-fied and relaxed-like. but as much as i love dinner here, brunch scratches my itch. i loooove their really, really good eggs benedict (many varieties—try 'em all!), but for me, it's all about the warm beignets. i can't find a word for how much they move me and i don't care if the powder sugar that wafts off the beignets coats my entire upper body. i'm better a little sweetened up anyway.

imbibe:
louisiana julep
obituary cocktail

devour:
oyster gratinée de bienville
crawfish pie
croque monsieur salad
pan-roasted rabbit
beignets! beignets!

sahagún

exquisite handmade chocolates

10 nw 16th avenue. between burnside and couch
503.274.7065 www.sahagunchocolates.com
wed - sat 10am - 6pm

opened in 2005. owner/chef: elizabeth montes
$: mc. visa
treats. first come, first served

northwest : nob hill > **e31**

some mornings lola will wake up and ask to have chocolate. i'll get all huffy and explain the importance of a good breakfast and then feed her cream of rice heaped with brown sugar. elizabeth has noted this same phenomenon—people who would say it was too early for chocolate but would be clutching a 62-ounce vanilla latte. so she got smart and created the benda mega morning chocolate. it looks like a quarter-sized "pill" and i guarantee it's healthier and better tasting than your weak coffee. and to wash it down? the *sahagún* hot chocolate which is ecstasy in a cup.

imbibe:
life-altering hot chocolate
rose soda

devour:
benda mega (mega pills) morning chocolate
jasmine truffles
cardamom palet
palomita papa
beautiful selection of bar chocolates

saint cupcake

the patron saint of sweet

nw: 407 nw 17th avenue. corner of flanders. 503.473.8760
se: 3300 se belmont. corner of 33rd. 503.473.8760
www.saintcupcake.com
tue - thu 9a - 8p fri 9a - 10p sat 10a - 10p sun 10a - 6p

opened in 2005. owners: jami and matthew curl   cupcake creator: jami curl
$: mc. visa
treats. first come, first served

northwest : nob hill > **e32**

i've heard some people complaining lately about cupcakes, like they are so 2005. people, come to your senses… cupcakes are forever. cupcakes are righteous. cupcakes are a staple of all well-rounded diets. look at the picture on this page of the little girl. she would tell you that a once-a-week (maybe twice) visit to *saint cupcake* is required for everyone under the age of 100. for my good health, i make sure to "take" a toasted coconut cream cupcake often, and lola highly recommends the hot fudge dot for clarity of thought. santé!

imbibe:
stumptown coffee
ice cold milk in a carton

devour:
cupcakes:
  red velvet
  fat elvis
  easter dots packed in egg cartons
cinnamon rolls (with saigon cinnamon)

the story of saint cupcake

The Story of Saint Cupcake is not widely known.

But few who remember it were the tale like the aroma of warm cinnamon rolls on a crisp fall day.

to the Baker's Daughter in the quiet Northern town where she lived. Not a morning passed without the sig

saucebox

pan asian and pacific island cuisine
214 sw broadway. corner of ankeny
503.241.3393 www.saucebox.com
tue - thu 4:30p - midnight fri - 4:30p - 2:30a sat 5p - 2:30a

opened in 1995. owners: bruce carey and joe rogers chef: chris israel
$$: all major credit cards accepted
dinner. late night. full bar. happy hour. reservations recommended

southwest : downtown > e33

when chris israel moved back to portland after being mr. nyc for almost a decade, i swear i heard bells ringing and foodies cheering. ding dong, one of portland's most beloved chefs had come back to town to take the helm once again at *saucebox*. just thinking about chris's version of hamachi and avocado had me singing the hallelujah chorus. you won't find the menu here radically different upon chris's return, but what you will find is that the food, which has always been good, is now just plain great—the flavors are clean and the ingredients gorgeous. hurrah.

imbibe:
monkey business
hitachino nest red rice ale

devour:
pupu platter for two
duck breast & long bean salad
sbx surf 'n' turf
red curry with vegetables
bird of paradise

savoy tavern and bistro

stylish neighborhood bistro with great american food

2500 se clinton street. corner of 25th

503.808.9999

bistro: tue - sun 5 - 10:30p fri - sat 5 - 11p bar: 5p - midnight

opened in 2005. owner: peter bro   chef: alton garcia

$$: all major credit cards accepted

dinner. late night. full bar. happy hour. first come, first served

southeast : clinton >

when i was a kid, i would go on family skiing trips. my pal janine and i, after taking two runs, would sneak into the lodge so we could beg saltine crackers and ketchup from the restaurant. something about those saltines rocked my boat, and today i still have a thing for them. so when i need my fix i'll just head over to the *savoy* and order the wisconsin tavern board—it's littered with saltines and just for good measure some sliced meats and cheeses. love it and love that the *savoy* offers good old hearty comfort food in a groovy atmosphere. it's the perfect mix.

imbibe:
eastside old fashioned
white port & soda

devour:
wisconsin tavern board
fried cheese curds
wedge salad
meatball sandwich
cherry bavarian cream pie

simpatica dining hall

fresh. local. seasonal

828 se ash avenue. corner of pine
503.679.7807 www.simpaticacatering.com
dinner: fri at 7:30p (one seating) sat at 7p (one seating)
sun "10 sandwiches" 5:30 - 9p brunch: 9a - 2p

opened in 2004. owner / chefs: benjamin dyer and john gorham chef: jason owens
$$: all major credit cards accepted
dinner. brunch. private dining. catering. viande meats at city market

southeast : industrial district > **e35**

in 1984 my band *matisse video* played one of their last gigs at pine street theater. flash forward to the early '90s, and i'm gyrating to the surf sounds of *satan's pilgrims* at pine street's new incarnation, la luna. forward again to 2006, i'm arriving for a dinner at 828 southeast ash for my first dinner at *simpatica dining hall*. it may no longer be a musical venue, but it's got the buzz and the verve still lingering which makes dining here a blast. whether it be dinner or the much-talked about brunch, the food is delish and the atmosphere eclectic and electric.

imbibe:
bloody mary
salty dog

devour:
classic eggs benny with roasted potatoes
fried chicken & waffles
crêpes with peas, bacon & crème fraiche
simpatica cheeseburger with cheddar & bacon
marionberry tart with lavender gelato

sohbet

coffee house and eclectic market
2710 n killingsworth. corner of burrage
503.735.3446
mon - fri 6a - 9p sat - sun 7:30a - 6p

opened in 2005. owner: david and julia santangelo
$: mc. visa
breakfast. lunch. dinner. treats. international coffees. first come, first served

north : nopo > **e36**

earlier this summer i began hearing about an enchant-ed little café called *sohbet*. so one day i dropped by to check it out. i walked in and was immediately taken with its warm vibe, light-filled space and appealing menu. i left knowing it would be a new favorite. i drove down the street about half a mile and got out of my car and a jiffy later a car pulled up at the curb. a lovely wom-an rolled down the window and asked what i thought about *sohbet*. this was julia, who gets my vote as the most creative market researcher i've ever met. my an-swer to her was, "fantastic!"

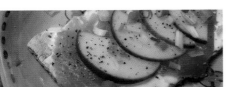

imbibe:
individually brewed:
turkish, cuban and vietnamese coffees

devour:
sohbet bresola plate
salmon crisp bread
jam crisp bread
vincent's turkey havarti roll-ups for kids
very yummy carrot cake

sweets etc.

candy and treats

7828 sw capitol highway. between 35th and 36th
503.293.0088 www.sweetsetc.com
mon - thu 11a - 8p fri 11a - 9p sat 10a - 9p sun 11a - 5p

opened in 1993. owner: tricia leahy
$: mc. visa
treats. first come, first served

southwest : multnomah village > e37

Gummi
Peaches
$6.50 / lb

Grapefruit
Slices
$6.50 / lb

Pink
Grapefruit
$6.50 / lb

Gummi
Fruit
Gies
6.25/lb

AFRA

SOUR APPLE

when i was growing up, my family would go to nes-kowin at the coast. there was a general store that we rode our bikes to so we could buy bags of penny candy: pixie sticks, sugar daddies, wax lips. my parents never worried about the amount of sugar we were devouring or about our teeth rotting away. in this era there's a lot o' sugar angst, so candy stores are hard to find. but lo' and behold, i discovered *sweets etc.*, an old-fashioned treats emporium in multnomah village. when i took lola there, she cried, "this is just like willy wonka's factory!" well, not quite—but it's pretty darn cool.

imbibe:
orchard blend spinner
chocolatté

devour:
handmade turtles
umpqua ice cream—any flavor!
gobs of old-style candies
candy pebbles
nik-l-nips

sydney's

a modern cup and saucer

1800 nw 16th avenue, suite 105. corner of thurman
503.241.4313
daily 7a - 6p

opened in 2005. owner: tim cox   chef: berkeley braden
$ - $$: all major credit cards accepted
breakfast. lunch. treats. coffee. first come, first served

northwest : under the bridge > **e38**

my family has a fascination with the fremont bridge. lola loves driving over it because it's the highest bridge in portland. i love driving and walking under it because i find there's a real beauty in the sweep of the huge support columns and the curves of the structure. so when *sydney's* opened up in the shadow of the fremont, i thought that was inspired. the space here feels lofty and modern and it's the perfect place to sit down with a cup of tea and one of bradley's scrumptious sandwiches and feel peaceful while the city zooms by overhead.

imbibe:
mocha piccante
tempest tea "springtime in paris"

devour:
baby leek & tomato soup
toasted brioche french toast
bl&t with housecured bacon
peanut butter & jelly sandwich with house-
    made peanut butter

tábor

authentic czech eatery

cart at sw fifth avenue. corner of stark
503.997.5467 www.schnitzelwich.com
mon - fri 10a - 3p

opened in 2004. owners: karel and monika vitek   chef: karel vitek
$: cash. check
breakfast. lunch. first come, first served

southwest : downtown > **e39**

people often make suggestions to me about places to eat. sometimes their faves don't quite match up to mine, but when my friend kevin told me about tábor, i was intrigued. first thing that piqued my interest: czech food. second thing: a cart in downtown. so i made plans to czech (sorry, couldn't help that) it out, but on the day i planned to go i had a tooth pulled. disaster! a couple of days later, i'd healed enough so that i could gum my food, so i took along my husband as official taster. the opinion: delicious! and when you're missing teeth, the goulash and dumplings fit the bill.

imbibe:
fresh carrot juice

devour:
original schnitzelwich
muenster cheese sandwich
bohemian goulash with dumplings
bramborak filled with spinach & ham
spaetzle (tue - thu)
german smoked sausage

the busy corner

grocery and café

4927 se 41st avenue. corner of raymond
503.777.5101
daily 7a - 7p siesta: mon - fri 2 - 4p

opened in 2005. owners: kyle and susan chaney
$ - $$: cash
breakfast. lunch. dinner. reservations required for friday night dinners

southeast : woodstock > e40

don't be fooled by the name. back in the day *the busy corner* might have been bustling, but now it's an oasis of calm that is just what the modern-day, over-burdened soul is in need of. put down your blackberry, your cell phone, your car-keys that sound an alarm when you lose them, and take a load off—an arugula salad with smoked trout and a glass of wine will remind you of your humanity. make sure to finish your mellow meal by 2pm, because that's siesta time. then on friday night return to sit under the stars at the *corner's* al fresco friday night dinner which is a picture of conviviality.

imbibe:
root beer float
a good glass of wine

devour:
poached eggs with greens & toast
toasted baguette with quince,
  tomato or nutella
arugula salad with smoked trout
pear & avocado bocadillos

the florida room

a little inner city vacation
435 n killingsworth. at commercial
503.287.5658 www.myspace.com//teamevil3
mon - fri 4p - midnight sat - sun noon - midnight

opened in 2006. owners: patty earley, suzy day and mike hanson
chef: mike hanson drinks geek: patty earley
$ - $$: mc. visa
dinner. full bar. first come, first served

north : nopo > **e41**

the world would be a happier place if all drinks were slushies. starting from day one, babies would be less fussy with slushy breast milk, toddlers giddy for slushy apple juice, teens stoked for slushy mountain dew, and adults—i'd be thrilled with slushy gin and tonics. the geniuses at *the florida room* figured out that slushies are king and installed a slushy machine—they'll slushy anything, though they won't guarantee that a slushy bloody mary will taste good. order a deep-fried avocado to go along with your drink, hang out on the patio and ooooh ahhhh, life is good.

imbibe:
mary mother of god (bloody mary)
key largo mojito slushy

devour:
pigs in a blanket
deep-fried avocado
tots with kickass fry spice
oyster shooters
voodoo donuts (on saturday)

valentine's

cool joint

232 sw ankeny. between 2nd and 3rd
503.248.1600
lunch: mon - fri noon - 4pm dinner: mon - sat 8p - close

opened in 2005. owner: jason bokros and liz haley
$: mc. visa
lunch. dinner. live music. first come, first served

southwest : old town > e42

i usually don't like to make sweeping proclamations about the best, the mostest, the coolest. but i'm breaking my own rule here by proclaiming *valentine's* egg salad sandwich to be the best best best sandwich i've had south of burnside. can't tell you the recipe, because it's top secret, but it includes eggs, some type of gooey blue cheese, chunks of cured meat and good, chewy grilled bread. stop me, i'm getting misty thinking about it. you can come for the sandwich, but stay here to soak up the atmosphere which is at once artful, musical (*clouds* is upstairs, see shop) and sociable.

imbibe:
bodegas piedmonte chardonnay
strawberry shasta

devour:
sandwiches:
  grilled egg salad (secret recipe)
  brie & greens
  reuben
ginger florentines

vindalho

spice route cuisine

2038 se clinton street. corner of 21st
503.467.4550 www.vindalho.com
tue - sat 5 - 10p

opened in 2005. owner/chef: david machado   chef de cuisine: david anderson
$$: all major credit cards accepted
dinner. full bar. private parties. reservations accepted for parties of six or more

southeast : clinton > **e43**

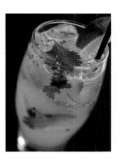

the last time i was in london with kevin, we headed straight for brick lane which is a long street jam-packed with indian, specifically bengali, restaurants. i don't know what it is about indian food in london, but the flavors just taste more vibrant there. if you want to taste a bit of that same vibrance closer to home, *vindahlo* is a good bet. david has taken the traditions of "spice route" cuisine and interpreted it with a modern touch which is lighter and full of flavor. it's akin to a bollywood movie that might feature orlando bloom instead of anil kapoor.

imbibe:
bahia breeze
walking man india pale ale

devour:
goan style mussels
green bean bahji
chicken malli kozhi
lamb boti kababs
cumin and fennel seed naan

wildwood

modern northwest cuisine

1221 nw 21st avenue. corner of overton
503.248.9663 www.wildwoodrestaurant.com
mon - sat 11:30a - 2:30p 5:30 - 9:30p sun 5 - 9p

opened in 1994. chef: cory schreiber
$$: all major credit cards accepted
lunch. dinner. full bar. reservations recommended

northwest : nob hill >

one of the reasons i'm married and have a child is that my friend dorie set me up on a blind date. when she was in her badgering stage of trying to set this up, her favorite place to bug me was at lunch at *wildwood*. we would prop ourselves up at the bar where i would have my beloved chicken romaine salad and listen to dorie extol kevin's virtues. now i'm mrs. kevin and lunch at *wildwood* is with him instead of the setter-upper. point of all of this is, good things happen at *wildwood* because cory's food was and still is the standard-bearer of pacific northwest cuisine.

imbibe:
chartreuse martini
2005 soter pinot noir rosé

devour:
gratin of local cardoons
baked cypress grove goat cheese
  with cherry purée
pan-seared alaskan halibut
frozen almond zabaglione with berries & cherries

about eat.shop

the first thing to know about the *eat.shop guides* is that they are the only guides dedicated to just eating and shopping. okay, we list some hotels, because we know that you need to sleep. and don't forget to whittle out some time for cultural activities—all of the businesses featured in the book are helmed by creative types who are highly influenced by the arts and sights of the cities they live in—culture is good for you.

the *eat.shop guides* feature approximately 90 carefully picked businesses, all of them homegrown and distinctive. some are small and some are big. some are posh and some are street. some are spendy and some require nothing more than pocket change. some are old school and some are shiny and new. some are hip and some are under-the-radar. point being, we like to feature a mix of places that are unique because you can feel the passionate vision of the owner(s) from the moment you step through their door, eat their food, touch their wares.

the guides each have one author. these authors have diverse backgrounds ranging from a graphic designer to a fashion stylist to a radio talk show host. each has the unique talent to research, write and photograph—which gives their book a distinctive voice and visual style. and a note on the photographs, they are shot with natural light and there is no propping or styling used—so what you see is the real deal. as for the copy, you already know we love these places because they're in the book, so we're not offering reviews or critiques or marketing blah blah. instead you get our experiential mini-stories.

enough explaining, here are a couple of things to remember when using this guide: remember that hours change seasonally, so always call or check the website before you go. we apologize if a featured business has closed—being small and local can be a rough road and some businesses don't make it—so use this book often and support the locals, they are the soul of the city. remember that items mentioned or pictures shown may not be available any longer, but there will most definitely be something even more fantastic available. finally, each guide has a two-year life span, and each new edition is different than the last—so collect them all! and if you don't have the past editions, not to worry. every business that has ever been featured in an *eat.shop guide* is archived on our website.

eat! shop! enjoy!

kaie wellman
creator and publisher of the *eat.shop guides*

kaie's notes

it's a little hard to believe that this is the fourth edition of *eat.shop.portland*. it seems like yesterday that i was cruising on i5 from san francisco to portland with a crazy idea rolling around in my head about creating a guide on independent eating and shopping in portland.

since that drive my life has been a long roller coaster ride of thrills. from those first thousand copies of *eat. shop.portland* that literally sold out in a day with me hawking them out of the back of my station wagon to my casual strategic planning for *eat.shop* growth—did i hear someone say i should do seattle? absolutely! los angeles? definitely! somewhere between all these exclamation marks, the series grew to thirteen cities, with the first city outside of the united states, paris, debuting this fall.

many people ask how i'm able to do all of this eating and shopping by myself, and the answer is i don't. i tried valiantly for two years, but then my expanding waistline and not-so-discretionary spending were getting out of hand. since then i've brought in some incredibly talented people to work on the guides. there's my fashion stylist pal agnes in los angeles; the only trained journalist in the group, anna in chicago; jan in rhode island who somehow juggles three kids, a radio show and a p.r. gig; and jon here in portland who owns jon's awesome business (www.jonsawesomebusiness.com). each of them research, write and photograph their title and then it's all turned over to me so i can mold it into the book you see.

what's up for the future? hopefully a long nap and some serious catching up with my tivo. but then after that it's back on the road—next year there will be new editions for los angeles, seattle, brooklyn, austin, san francisco and chicago. and then i'll be adding on minneapolis, east bay (san francisco), atlanta, new orleans, charlotte and london.

and remember, just because you are buying this new edition of *eat.shop.portland*, don't relinquish your last edition (or the 2nd or 1st edition). since there is only room for 90 businesses in each edition, you need to keep all the books—think of it as the *eat.shop* library. and if you need to know if the businesses are still open or if they have moved, no problem. just visit the website *www.eatshopguides.com* where you will find all the updated information you might need.

eat.shop.enjoy.

k

kaie wellman
kaie@eatshopguides.com
july 2006

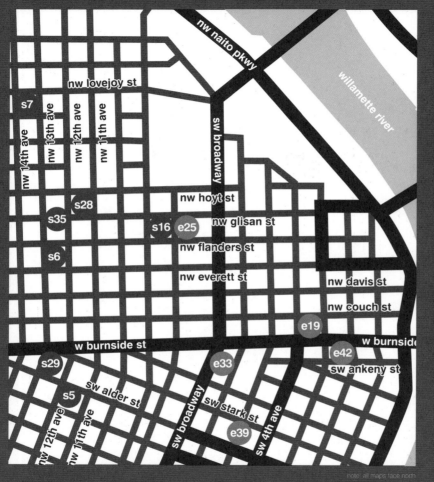

eat

e19 > good taste restaurant
e25 > park kitchen
e33 > saucebox
e39 > tabor
e42 > valentine's

shop

s5 > canoe
s6 > cargo
s7 > cheeky b
s16 > hive
s28 > oblation papers & press
s29 > odessa
s35 > possession

note: all maps face north

downtown/pearl district/old town

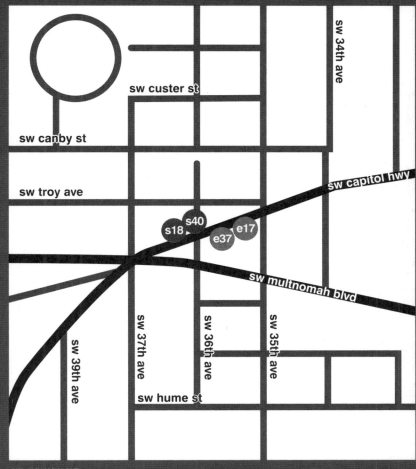

eat

e17 > fat city cafe
e37 > sweets etc

shop

s18 > indigo traders
s40 > switch shoes

sw canby st

sw custer st

sw troy ave

sw capitol hwy

s18 s40 e37 e17

sw multnomah blvd

sw 34th ave

sw 39th ave

sw 37th ave

sw 36th ave

sw 35th ave

sw hume st

note: all maps face north

multnomah village

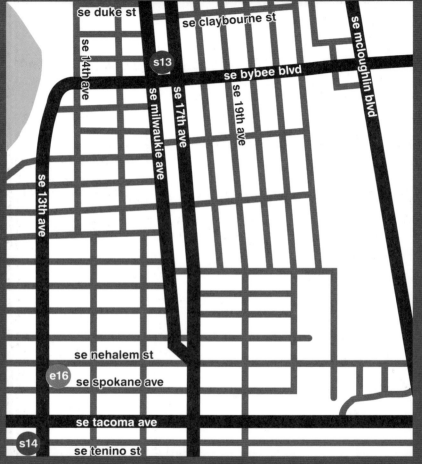

eat

e16 > curds & whey

shop

s13 > fuchsia
s14 > gr scrub

note: all maps face north

sellwood / westmoreland

eat

e10 > café castagna
e11 > castagna
e23 > nostrana
e26 > pastaworks
e27 > pix patisserie
e28 > pok pok
e34 > savoy
e40 > the busy corner
e43 > vindahlo

shop

s24 > missing link
s27 > muse art & design
s33 > polliwog

southeast quadrant

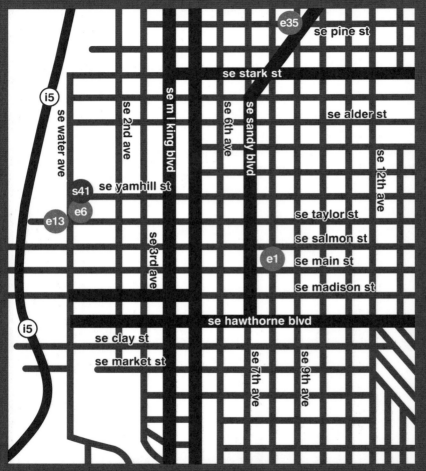

eat

e1 > acme
e6 > bakery bar
e13 > clarklewis
e35 > simpatica

shop

s41 > the lippman
company

note: all maps face north

eastside industrial

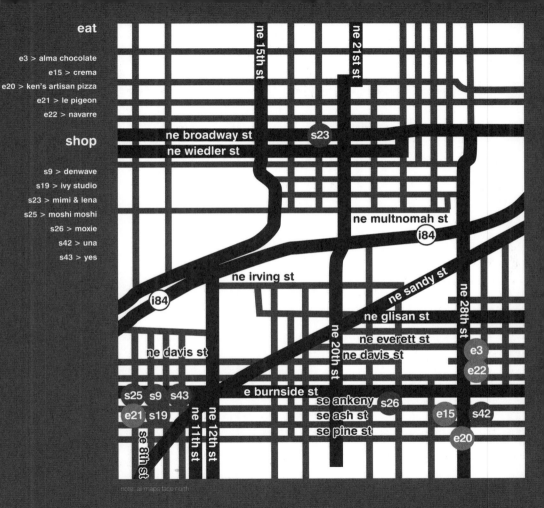

eat

e3 > alma chocolate
e15 > crema
e20 > ken's artisan pizza
e21 > le pigeon
e22 > navarre

shop

s9 > denwave
s19 > ivy studio
s23 > mimi & lena
s25 > moshi moshi
s26 > moxie
s42 > una
s43 > yes

note: all maps face north

lower burnside / 28th

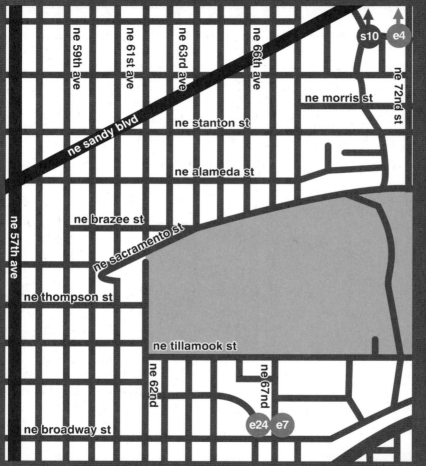

eat

e4 > annie's donuts
e7 > binh minh
bakery & deli
e24 > pacific
supermarket

shop

s10 > ed's house
of gems

note: all maps face north

rose city

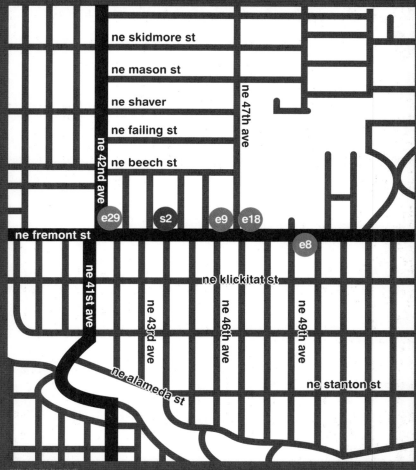

eat

e8 > blue moose cafe
e9 > bumblekiss
e18 > foxfire teas
e29 > ristretto roasters

shop

s2 > bella flora studio

ne skidmore st

ne mason st

ne shaver

ne failing st

ne beech st

ne 47th ave

ne 42nd ave

e29   s2   e9   e18

ne fremont st

e8

ne 41st ave

ne klickitat st

ne 43rd ave

ne 46th ave

ne 49th ave

ne alameda st

ne stanton st

note: all maps face north

beaumont village / irvington

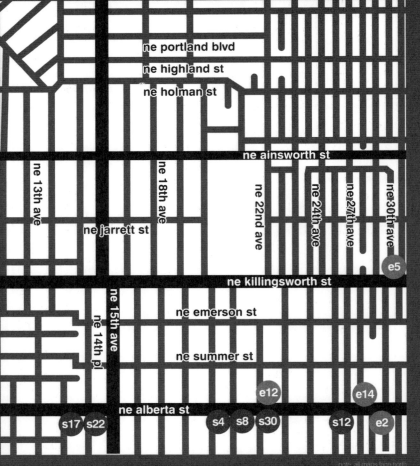

eat

e2 > alberta street oyster bar & grill
e5 > autentica
e12 > ciao vito
e14 > cork

shop

s4 > bolt
s8 > close knit
s12 > foundation garments
s17 > imp
s22 > mabel & zora
s30 > office

alberta / killingsworth

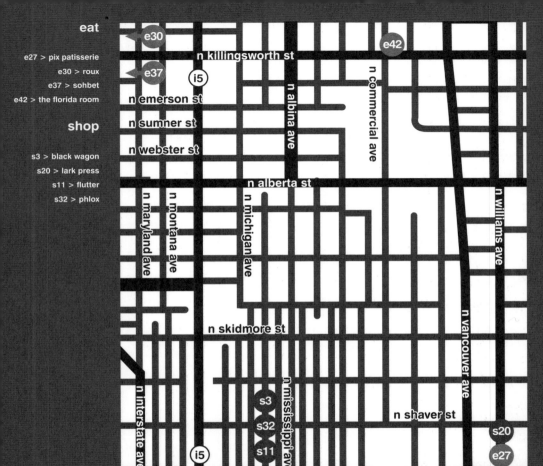

eat

e27 > pix patisserie
e30 > roux
e37 > sohbet
e42 > the florida room

shop

s3 > black wagon
s20 > lark press
s11 > flutter
s32 > phlox

mississippi / nopo

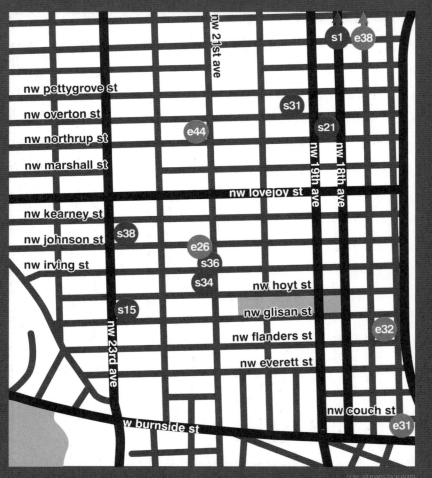

eat

e26 > pastaworks
e31 > sahagun
e32 > saint cupcake
e38 > sydney's
e44 > wildwood

shop

s1 > bedford brown
s15 > hello portland
s21 > le train bleu
s31 > opal
s34 > portland modern
s36 > quinn in the city
s38 > souchi

northwest / nob hill

kaie's twenty favorite things

eat

1 > the hot chocolate at *sahagun*

2 > the khao soi kai at *pok pok*

3 > the roasted duck with egg noodles at *good taste restaurant*

4 > the bone marrow & carmelized onion sandwich at *le pigeon*

5 > the chef's tasting menu at *park kitchen*

6 > the roasted duck with egg noodles at *good taste restaurant*

7 > the beignets at *roux*

8 > the turkish coffee at *sohbet*

9 > the alcoholic slushies at *the florida room*

10 > the egg salad sandwich at *valentine's*

shop

11 > the fairy furniture at *bella flora studio*

12 > the jack spade ping-pong paddle covers at *office*

13 > the chemex water kettle at *canoe*

14 > the cool korean line of paper goods at *cheeky b*

15 > the she-bible lady's onesie at *denwave*

16 > the 1930's deauville chairs at *flutter*

17 > the mystic mop at *gr scrub*

18 > the nicholas k coat at *le train bleu*

19 > the do-it-yourself munny at *missing link*

20 > the tibi tunics and dresses at *una*

notes

where to lay your weary head

there's many great places to stay in portland, but here's a couple of my picks:

hotel deluxe
729 sw fifth avenue
503.219.2094
www.hoteldeluxeportland.com
standard double: $189- $259
restaurant/bar: gracie's and the driftwood room

hotel lucia
400 sw broadway
503.22.1717
www.hotellucia.com
standard double: $185 - $255
restaurant: typhoon!

the ace hotel
1022 sw stark street
503.228.2277
www.acehotel.com
standard double with shared bath: $85
king suite: $225
restaurant/bar: the clyde opening early 2007

the jupiter hotel
800 east burnside street
503.230.9200
www.jupiterhotel.com
standard double: $124 - $154
restaurant/bar: doug fir

bedford brown

objects for home and garden

1825 nw vaughn. corner of 18th
503.227.7755 www.bedfordbrown.com
tue - sat 10a - 5p

opened in 2003. owners: steve bedford and henry brown
all major credit cards accepted
interior and exterior design services. holiday installations. staging

northwest : under the bridge > **s1**

i'm embarassed to say this, but no matter what i do, i seem to be the grim reaper for plants. i love plants, but they just seem to shrivel under my not-so-watchful eye. so when i discovered the entire room of faux plants at *bedford brown*, i was really excited. not only do they look unbelievably real, they are un-killable! if you are not like me, and have a green thumb, there are scads of living plants here that will tickle your fancy also. everything at *bedford brown* is just plain gorgeous, it's a decorating garden of paradise that will inspire you from the moment you enter.

covet:
everything in the greenhouse
big vases to fill with super realistic faux plants
upholstered furniture
beautiful lamps
illuminata oculatum apothecary candles
cool lanterns
orchids, orchids, orchids
modern outdoor furniture

bella flora studio

floral artistry and more
4439 ne fremont street. between 44th and 45th
503.866.3009 www.bellaflorastudio.com
mon - sat 11a - 5p (hours vary)

opened in 1996. owner: elaine falbo
cash. check
custom designs

northeast : beaumont village > **s2**

for years now i have walked by *bella flora* and wondered what magic existed behind the closed doors. one gorgeous day this past summer i finally entered the enchanted realm. in the middle of the tiny room sat elaine, patiently gluing together tiny twigs to create a fairy chair. her work is so beautiful, it makes you catch your breath. poke around and you'll discover rainbow-toned head crowns, romantic vintage gowns and spectacular woven pussy willow vases that are each one of a kind. everything that elaine touches is spun gold and will become a treasured family heirloom.

covet:
fairy furniture: beds, chairs & tables
fairy wings
woven pussy willow baskets & wreaths
luscious vintage dresses
enchanting head crowns
vintage chinese lanterns
sparkly, sequined dancing skirts

109

black wagon

style destination for kids and parents

3964 n mississippi avenue. corner of shaver
503.916.0000 / 866.916.004 (toll free) www.blackwagon.com
mon - sat 11a - 7p sun 11p - 5p

opened in 2006. owner: sarah s. shaoul
mc. visa
online shopping. special orders. personal shopping. alterations/tailoring

northeast : mississippi > s3

in the '70s in portland, there was one place to get groovy clothing for kids: *youngland*. going there was a big deal, but i didn't mind because i got fancy dresses and there might have been lollipops involved. pdx kids today have a plethora of places to get fab duds, but one of coolest is the spankin' new *black wagon*. sarah is a retail legend in portland—for years she had *retread threads*, but then along came her son and her focus shifted to the mini-set. now her wickedly good fashion sense is benefiting the kiddos and someday they'll talk about the first time they went to *black wagon*.

covet:
egg & avocado screen-printed knit suits
harajuku lovers by gwen stefani
dirty laundry handmade t's & onesies
salvor t's
vans toddler classics
amy tangerine handmade tie onesie
no added sugar's lock up your daughter t's

bolt

neighborhood fabric boutique
2136 ne alberta street. corner of 22nd
503.287.bolt(2658) www.boltfabricboutique.com
tue - fri 10a - 6p sat 10a - 5p sun 11a - 4p

opened in 2005. owner: gina cadenasso
mc. visa
classes

northeast : alberta > **s4**

back when i had a dorothy hamill haircut, i took a sewing class at meier & frank. my friend susan and i made cotton a-line skirts and simple t's with matching neck scarves. we did a little fashion show of our creations, and boy, did i feel chic. tragically, that was the end of my sewing career. but walking into *bolt* made me want to start again. the fabrics here are soooo darn cool that *bolt* alone could make the sewing trend as big as the knitting and crafting trends. the colors are brilliant, the patterns fresh—watch out *project runway*, i'm going to sew an entire new wardrobe for myself.

covet:
fabrics:
   mirror ball dot by michael miller
   all amy butler
   great soft flannels
   denyse schmidt for free spirit
metallic embroidery floss
farmer's market tote pattern

canoe

simple, beautiful, functional objects
1136 sw alder. corner of 12th
503.889.8545 www.canoeonline.net
tue - sat 10a - 6p sun noon - 5p

opened in 2005. owners: sean igo and craig olson
mc. visa
online shopping. special orders

southwest : downtown > s5

i have a little rule for myself when i'm working on these guides: no buying allowed. often the business owners see me grimacing or twitching as i'm refraining from the need to purchase. but at *canoe*, i broke down—in a big way. i began with an egg-shaped bird feeder for my mother, then i just started piling things at the register. sean was valiantly trying to gift-wrap my ever-growing mound but soon was begging for mercy. i couldn't stop because *canoe* is a candyland for anybody who loves good design. there's nothing here i don't want—so sean, beware... i'll be back with a shopping cart.

covet:
heath ceramics
kristian vedel birds
tivoli audio model one radio
chemex water kettle & coffee pot
joe cariati glass
beautiful design books
cedar sake cups

cargo

antiques, new furniture and artifacts from asia and beyond
380 nw 13th avenue. between everett and flanders
503.209.8346 / 503.243.7804 www.cargoinc.com
daily 11am - 6pm

opened in 1995. owner: patty merrill
all major credit cards accepted

northwest : pearl district > **s6**

whenever i'm in asia, i can't help but think about patty merrill. i'm pretty sure that as i'm flying into singapore, she's stomping around china or indonesia somewhere, discovering yet more incredible objects that she will bring back to her fan-freaking-tastic store *cargo*. this woman is a discoverer par excellence and every time i think that there's no way i can be suprised anymore, all i have to do is visit *cargo,* and patty will have found some incredible object from bali or malaysia that will have my head spinning.

covet:
yorubu beaded chair
gobs of brightly painted furniture
empress robe from beijing
balinese tin stacking baskets
chubby java stone pigs
stools of all shapes & sizes
groovy beaded belts
javanese dancing puppets

cheeky b

urban life accessories store

906 nw 14th avenue. corner of kearney
503.274.0229 www.cheekyboutique.com
mon - sat 10a - 7p sun 10a - 5p

opened in 2004. owner: becca smith
mc. visa. amex
wish lists. gift registries. personal shopping. gift baskets

northwest : pearl district > **s7**

i would like to think that i'm somewhat in the know about groovy toys, but when i was walking around *cheeky b* recently, i asked becca to point out some of her hot sellers and she went right to the vacuum-packed furilla. coming from an upbringing in the '70s when vacuum-packing was in its prime, i immediately thought the furilla was pretty darn cool. but i had to test this with different age brackets, and here are the results: the under 6's—cool! the under 15's—cool! the under 30's—cool! the over 50's—what is it? market research says: the furilla should top your gift-giving list.

covet:
mmmg paper goods & accessories
  (cool korean line)
subversive cross stitch by julie jackson
the orange furilla
beth myrick stenciled record albums
amuse bouche melamine nesting bowls
gyms pac computer bags
fred ice kabobs

close knit

the neigborhood yarn shop
2140 ne alberta street. corner of 22nd
503.288.4568 www.closeknitportland.com
tue 10a - 6p wed 10a -10p thu - fri 10a - 6p sat 10a - 5p sun 11a - 4p

opened in 2005. owner: sally palin
all major credit cards accepted
loads of good classes

northeast : alberta > s8

this summer i was on vacation on the mckenzie river with a group of friends, and in the afternoon the ladies would gather in a common area on blankets and many of them would pull out their knitting projects—even the kids were hanging out doing groovy yarn "stars." you might say this was bucolic, except i ruined the pretty picture by leafing through trashy magazines while wearing my obscenely pink, paris hilton shades. i obviously needed to go get some *close knit* training. sally's not only got fantastic yarns, but also some cool classes like how to knit a light summer bobble hat. sign me up!

covet:
bamboo yarns
imperial stock ranch yarns
soy silk yarns
habu stainless steel & linen paper yarns
manos del uruguay hand-spun yarns
array of knitted bags that you can learn to knit!
cool lucite bag handles
mason dixon knitting: the curious knitters guide

denwave

modern clothing, jewelry and accessories
811 e burnside street suite 113. corner of 8th avenue
503.233.3189 www.denwave.com
wed - sun noon - 7pm

opened in 2004. owners: hazel cox and genevieve dellinger
all major credit cards accepted
custom jewelry and clothing

northeast : lower burnside > **s9**

the portland of today is chameleon-like... it's ever-changing, but its colors are always true. part of this landscape includes a few visionary retailers who have brought a fresh, modern style into play. some of these places started small but gradually have been able to transform their spaces into more fully realized environments. *denwave* is a part of this. originally named *fix*, the store began with a rawer edge. today, the interior design, merchandising and fixturing have been gorgeously updated with a chic, urban vibe so you feel like you're shopping in brooklyn or even better, brussels.

covet:
hazel cox jewelry
genevieve dellinger clothing
intentions perfume by caitlyn davies
nature vs. future clothing
john blasioli men's clothing
she-bible lady's onesie
moonblood hand-dyed & silkscreened t's
obey coats'& jackets

123

ed's house of gems

classic rock and gem shop
7712 ne sandy boulevard. corner of 77th
503.284.8990 www.edshouseofgems.com
mon - fri 9a - 5:30p fri - sat 9a - 5p

opened in 1956
mc. visa

northeast : rose city > **s10**

a couple of months ago, lola began to get interested in collecting rocks. in the time since, she's gathered some real doozies: thundereggs, fossils, minerals that look like precious gems. by far her favorite place to shop is *ed's house of gems*. it's easy to see why—*ed's* is just so darn cool that both kids and adults alike walk in and are soon yapping away about trilobites and obsidian, cavansite and olivine. for fifty years portlanders have come here, and i imagine that for fifty more this will be a destination not only for the rock-hound types, but also for people looking for gifts and jewelry.

covet:
7-million-year-old sand dollar fossils
450-million-year-old trilobite
gorgeous blazing blue azurite
carnelian marbles
titanium clusters
big chunks of obsidian
shells! gems!
casting equipment

flutter

a delightful disarray of found objects and clutter

3948 n mississippi avenue. between shaver and failing
503.288.1649 www.flutterclutter.com
tue - sat 11a - 6p sun 11a - 4p

opened in 2006. owner: cindy rokoff
mc. visa
online shopping

northeast : mississippi > **s11**

there are certain places that from the moment you enter, you know you're not going to want to leave. that's *flutter* for me. cindy has created the most delightful, magical world filled with objects both old and new that have been put on this earth for me to buy. and because i don't want to be hopelessly narcissistic, i want you to buy things here also—mainly so there will be more room for cindy to discover and stock more cool, quirky items. she's got such a great eye that after you make your puchases, you'll beg her to come home with you and tell you just the right spots to put them in.

covet:
vintage plateware
a multitude of bird-related items
1930s deauville chairs
yummy european soaps
parisian saints
vintage aprons
streamline trains & racecars
dum dums!

foundation garments

independent clothing and accessories from north america

2712 ne alberta street. corner of 27th
503.282.2763 www.foundationgarmentsinc.com
mon - sat 11a - 7p sun noon - 6p

opened in 2006. owner: heidi carlson
mc. visa
online shopping

northeast : alberta > **s12**

lola is constantly bugging me to wear fancier under-wear and bras. at five, she already sees that cool un-dies are where it's at—so i know she would be egging me on to buy the "dainties" at *foundation garments*. you would not be embarassed wearing these if your skirt got windblown around your ears. and that skirt should also be bought at *foundation* along with the rest of your wardrobe. heidi is stocking some of the freshest inde-pendent designers in the nation. everything here feels modern with a slight avant-garde twist and the price-point is right on for even the most budget minded.

covet:
troy linden silkscreen shirts, t's & ties
blood is the new black t's
ship to shore "dainties"
kitchen orange dresses
amet & sasha skirts & tops
day-lab jewelry
bookhou design linen bags

fuchsia

nice things for you and your home
6658 se milwaukie. a block north from bybee
503.232.3737 www.fuchsiastyle.com
mon - sat 10a - 6p sun 11a - 5p

opened in 2006. owner: anne reis
mc. visa

southeast : westmoreland > s13

i'll admit it—i am under-accessorized. i wear three simple thin wedding bands and a platinum "engagement" bracelet. when i feel like busting out, i'll sport a pair of earrings. my supersta' stylist lola (see previous page) bugs me often to get a bit more bling on. if i decide to follow her advice, i'll be heading straight for *fuchsia*. anne has created a vibrant environment of treasures which to not only adorn yourself, but your home. the jewelry choices range from simple and chic to bejeweled yet understated. and the home accessories will undoubtedly bring some sparkle to your abode.

covet:
minoux handcrafted jewelry
david aubrey jewelry
betty carré haute-fantasie 18k gold jewelry
michael michaud table art pewter
fringe studio vases & dishes
rosanna pottery
recycled paper handbags

131

gr scrub

all manner of materials and tools for clean house
8235 se 13th avenue #12. between tenino and umatilla
503.236.8986 www.grscrub.com
tue noon - 5p wed - sat 11a - 5p sun noon - 4p

opened in 2006. owner: glenn recchia
mc. visa
clean classes. personal cleaning training

southeast : sellwood > s14

for weeks i have been surveying the tragic state of my home. i'm fixated on the three inches of grime, dust and the wafting fur of two dogs and a pissed-off long-haired cat. my next free moment, i'm heading to *gr scrubb*—a mecca for cleanies, or those who wish they were, like me. glenn is a guru when it comes to spotless. for years he cleaned swanky houses in the bay area, and now he's taken that knowledge and put it into *gr scrub* which has everything you need for a shining household. note: glenn has a multitude of helpful hints, so take time to chat with him. he's portland's cleaning therapist.

covet:
glenn says you must have:
  bon ami original formula
  the mystic mop
albert einstein's "no more smelly shoes"
vaska "out damn spot" remover
old craftsmen's white ring spot remover
brush by daniel rozensztroch and shiri slavin
non-mildewing head & body scrubber

hello portland

fun lifestyle and gift boutique

525 nw 23rd avenue. between hoyt and glisan
503.274.0771 www.shophello.com
daily 10am - 8pm

opened in 2005. owners: mr and mrs korn
all major credit cards accepted
online shopping.

northwest : nob hill > s15

i'm a sucker for gifty-type stores. one evening, not soon after *hello portland* opened, i had my face plastered to their windows. when i realized they were closed, i got a bit depressed because i had wallet in hand, ready to buy buy buy. it was a happy day for me when i was finally able to walk into the store—it was so much better than my late night window-shopping spree. there were well-designed goodies everywhere, and many fantastic items that were completely new to my universe, like the udder baby bottle. cachink! put two in basket, perfect for baby shower gifts. *hello world* is shopping bliss.

covet:
pop ink culinary art plates
candeloo! rechargeable lamps
oxo design rabbit fm radio
blue q cutie fruit bag
vice versa "udder" baby bottle
pod blaster stereo travel case
party partners loot bags
paint-by-numbers kit

hive

modern design for the home

820 nw glisan. corner of 9th
503.242.1967 www.hivemodern.com
mon - sat 11a - 6p

opened in 2002. owner: patrick fisher
all major credit cards accepted
online shopping

northwest : pearl district > **s16**

does everybody have a fantasy home? is it modern? do you spend hours looking at design magazines like *dwell*, ripping out ideas to put in your "i will have this home, this furniture and these appliances someday" file? if you answered yes to all of the above, then *hive* is your type of store. patrick was one of the first retailers in portland to focus purely on modern design for the home, and if i had my druthers, not only my future fantasy home, but my existing abode would be filled with pieces from here. i'll take a cassina sectional, some blu dot shelving and a couple of eames chairs, please.

covet:
furniture:
  cassina
  kartell
  herman miller
  fritz hanson
alessi everything
iittalia glass
flos lighting

imp

fun and joy for your home and body
1422 ne alberta. between 14th and 15th
503.282.7467 www.imponalberta.com
tue - sun 11a - 6p fri 11a - 7p sun 11a - 4p

opened in 2005. owner: christine karhi
all major credit cards accepted
custom orders

northeast : alberta > s17

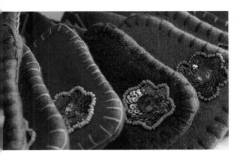

imp has two dictionary definitions: a mischievous child and a small demon. as some of you know, this can be one in the same. but there should be a third definition: a sweet, spirited boutique. even though i featured *imp* in the last edition, i still have people ask me if i know about "this wonderful store on alberta." that's because everybody feels that *imp* is their own special discovery, and christine's warm personality makes everybody feel like they're a friend. and does she have an eye for the good stuff? oh yeah, from groovy aprons to funky jewelry, *imp* has got just what you need.

covet:
diana fayt ceramics
lily lambert jewelry & scents
classic hardware jewelry
edge wrap skirts, aprons & t's
pine cone hill pj's & caftans
david fussenegger cotton blankets
shadow light by tord boontje
eloquent ink cards & wrapping papers

indigo traders

fine mediterranean textiles and interiors
7881 sw capitol highway. corner of 36th
503.780.2422 www.indigotraders.com
tue - sat 10a - 6p sun 11a - 4p

opened in 2003. owners: samir naser and karla bean
mc. visa
gift registry. in-home consultation. corporate gifting. special orders

southwest : multnomah village > **s18**

years ago, my brother lived in spain, and when i would visit him we would travel to morocco. through my brother i gained a love for the crafts of the region: the lanterns, the pottery, the jewel-like tea glasses. when glenn at *gr scrub* told me i would find these things and more at *indigo traders*, i got on my magic carpet and swooped over. samir and karla carry some gorgeous moroccan goods, but what i was really swooning over were the turkish towels and syrian bedding. the towels are super absorent and last forever and the syrian bedding is an arabian nights fantasy.

covet:
turkish towels
syrian bedding
palestinian hand-embroidered pillows
moroccan leather ottomans
hand-painted turkish ceramics
moroccan tea glasses & lanterns
olive oil soaps from all over the world

ivy studio

a modern-day gift store
800 e burnside street. between 8th and 9th
503.231.7400 www.theivystudio.com
sun - mon 10a - 3p tue - thu 10a - 7p fri - sat 10a - 8p

opened in 2005. owners: luke and erika smalley
all major credit cards accepted
online shopping. custom order

northeast : lower burnside > s19

i have noticed in my travels for these guides that many of the hotels i stay in don't have gift stores. what's up? it's all about the honor-bar now, but hotel folk, i want you to know… that just doesn't cut it. there's gotta be a groovy little store. *ivy studio*, which is part of the jupiter hotel complex, is just the ticket. there's mod mags, stylish books and old-school candy for the lounging hours. then for the serious shoppers, there's everything from a one-of-a-kind bike to lomo cameras. i suggest getting lubricated next door at *doug fir,* then when you buy a dozen guy burwell posters, you'll feel no pain.

covet:
limited-edition hand-silkscreened
   concert posters by guy burwell & mike king
red bat press letterpress cards
lomography cameras
marimekko umbrellas
old-school candy
harajuku lovers clothing for kids & adults
books, books, books

lark press

letterpress printing and more
3901 n williams avenue. between failing and shaver
503.546.9930 www.larkpress.com
wed - sat 11a - 6p sun noon - 5p

opened in 2005. owner: jean sammis
mc. visa
custom orders

northeast : nopo > **s20**

i am forever fascinated with all things letterpress. to this day, i regret not buying a press from a printer who was getting away from the old school of printing. but then i remembered you need to have somewhere to put your two-ton machine. right. didn't have that place, so i'll just go to *lark press* instead and watch jean in action as she creates her whimsical line of cards and invites. you can work with her on custom designs for whatever event might be happening next in your life or buy from the other letterpressed lines or paper goods she carries. either way, you'll leave with something good.

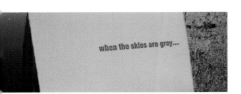

when the skies are grey...

covet:
lark press cards & invites
little lark silkscreened baby clothes
snow & graham papers
robot candy coasters & sweet little charms
waste not paper company cards
peculiar pair press cards
k.g. earthings jewelry

le train bleu

romantic women's clothing with an edge
1822 nw overton street. between 18th and 19th
503.343.5140 www.letrainbleu.com
tue - sat noon - 5p

opened in 2006. owner: bria phillips
all major credit cards accepted
online shopping (free shipping for portland residents). private parties

northwest : nob hill > **s21**

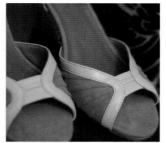

i love nothing better than the off-the-beaten-path gem. i had heard about *le train bleu*, but when i went to visit i found myself wondering how a clothing store could be located on a residential street in northwest. i drove by the address a couple of times, but all i saw was a house. then i decided to slow down and really open my eyes—and i noticed that the porch light said *le train bleu*. ahhhh, brilliant subtlety. entering was even more pleasing. i wanted to throw down the camera and fill my arms with the deliciously chic clothing and shoes. *l'amour*.

covet:
clothing:
  nicholas k
  erotokritos
  bi la li
  vena cava
melanie dezon shoes & clutches
pink shoes
bliss lau bags

mabel and zora

a ladies' boutique

1468 ne alberta street. corner of 14th
503.335.6169
tue - sun 11a - 7p

opened in 2006. owner: tiffanee bean
mc. visa

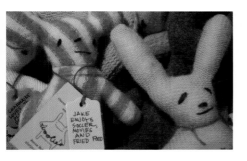

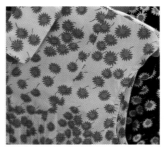

i was walking down alberta one day this summer and i looked up to see a sign for *mabel and zora*. double take. a new boutique on alberta? yippee. i went in and found a cute-as-a-button place that will be a spot of sunshine in the portland retail scene. the day i visited was their first official day open and within the first ten minutes i was there, the place was filled with eager shoppers. giddy with ultra-affordable prices and sweetly feminine clothes the ladies were jockeying for dressing-room time. but i wanted to tell them, don't bother—you all look scrumptious.

covet:
lani dresses
kirstin crowley jewelry
san diego hats & bags
retro rags t's
catherine manuell luggage
kicklet kreations jewelry
jenna robertsons woolies

mimi & lena

stylish clothing for women and children
1914 ne broadway. between 19th and 20th
503.224.7736 www.mimiandlena.com
mon - sat 10a - 6p sun noon - 5p

opened in 1991. owner: julie ann lovestrand
all major credit cards accepted
special orders. wardrobing

northeast : irvington > s23

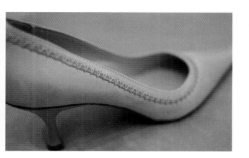

this summer i was at a picnic for my daughter's new school, and i got to talking to a really lovely woman, julie ann. after a bit someone mentioned the *eat.shop guides* and she looked at me and said, "you're the *eat.shop* lady?" guilty. she confessed that she owned *mimi & lena*, to which i replied, "you're the *mimi & lena* lady?" then it was just a big old lovefest—everybody had to step back from the glow of mutual admiration. julie ann's store is beloved by the ladies of portland because there's always the perfect modern mix of clothing not only for women, but also for children.

covet:
diane von furstenberg
erica tanov
rachel mara
tocca
jean paul gaultier jeans
tree
super suite seventy seven
danielle welmond jewelry

missing link

toys. books. art.
3314 se belmont street. between 33rd and 39th
503.235.0032 www.missinglinktoys.com
daily noon - 7p

opened in 2005
mc. visa
online shopping. events. gallery

southeast : belmont > **s24**

do you know the difference between urban vinyl and art toys? no? me neither. my relatively uneducated guess is that they are one and the same, but if you really wanted to get the lowdown, you should head to *missing link*. for all those who collect or are just fans of this modern, urban toy-as-sculpture movement, *missing link* is most definitely a go-to spot where there's dunny's a-plenty—my fave are the toys by seminal '80s nyc graffiti artist futura 2000. not so into the toys, but dig the style? no problem, there are t's and books and mags that will satisfy.

covet:
kid robot exclusive dunny's
clutter magazine
unkl brand hazmapo
gama-go t's
camille rose garcia dolls
the king by rich koslowski
nosferatu by futura 2000
do-it-yourself munny

moshi moshi

japanese cute stuff
811 e burnside street. between 8th and 9th
503.233.3993 www.moshi-moshi.com
wed - sun 11a - 7p

opened in 2005. owner: billy galaxy
mc. visa
online shopping

northeast : lower burnside > **s25**

in the summer of 1986, i lived in tokyo where i spent many hours wandering through the corriders of shinjuku and roppongi. my favorite places to shop would be the tiny little stores that were packed with groovy things like coin purses and mini-pens with nonsensical english sayings on them. not only did this stuff crack me up, but the design was brilliant. flash forward twenty years later to portland, and i'm in *moshi moshi* and it's almost as good as being in tokyo. billy's got stuff here that you can't find outside of japan—need some japanese toe socks? this is where to come.

covet:
mini - k t's
aranzi aronzo everything
swimmer everything
cell phone charms
mountain mountain everything
mind sock toe socks
zillions of cool stickers

moxie

boutique without the boutique prices

2400 e burnside. corner of 24th
503.29moxie (296.6943) www.moxiepdx.com
tue - sat 11a - 7p sun noon - 5p

opened in 2005. owners: denise bell and sandra loewe
mc. visa
shopping parties

northeast : burnside > s26

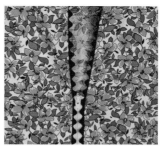

everytime i think of *moxie*, i always think about one of portland's all-time great party bands, *moxie love crux*. i've made the connection between the two, not just because of the shared name, but because the hip chicks that would be grooving to the *moxie love crux* sound would be the type to sport the *moxie* **(the store)** look: vintage-inspired, but with an urban edge. if this is your style, and there's a good chance it is because you live in portland, then *moxie* should be your style headquarters.

covet:
the people have spoken clothing
level 99 wide-leg jeans
ben sherman tops
bella sisters 99% recycled hoodie blazer
ric rac dress
zachary pryor jewelry
shoes!

muse art & design

essentials for everyday artist

4224 se hawthorne blvd. between 42nd and 43rd
503.231.8704 www.museartanddesign.com
mon - sat 10a - 6p sun noon - 5p

opened in 2005. owner: peter rossing
all major credit cards accepted
reference library. display space for local artists. frequent buyer program
sketchbook walks. artist discussion groups

southeast : hawthorne > **s27**

i love art stores. i could spend hours looking at the rainbow of oil paints or deciding what type of pen is ultimate. but sometimes i feel a bit overwhelmed by big stores, so i flip out and leave with nothing. to soothe my artistic self, i think i'll head to *muse art & design*, which is just the right size. you'll find everything you need here whether you are a painter, a designer, an illustrator, a hobbyist or all of the above. and while you're picking up your supplies, check out all of the perks peter has to offer the local artist from sketchbook walks to a reference library, he's covered all the bases.

covet:
williamsburg handmade oil colors
brushes, brushes, brushes
lyra color giant pencils
hand-crafted papers
strathmore windpower drawing paper
fan sumi set
mosaic materials

oblation papers & press

european-style paper boutique and letterpress and hand papermaking shop

pearl: 516 nw 12th avenue. between glisan and hoyt. 503.223.1093
bridgeport village: 7459 sw bridgeport road. 503.968.7131
www.oblationpapers.com
nw: mon - sat 10a - 6p sun noon - 5p bv: mon - sat 10a - 8p sun 11a - 5p

opened in 1989. owners: ron and jennifer rich
all major credit cards accepted
online ordering. custom letterpress and printing

are there stores that you love so much that you feel like you know them inside and out? this is how i feel about *oblation*. i know without a doubt that i'll find gorgeous cards and perfect gifts there. but the last time i visited, i was thrown for a loop. i started discovering things i had never seen or known about before. did you know they have a really cool book-binding service where they create pre-bound albums that you can then customize (at home) with your own cover paper choice? after i saw this, i knew it was finally time to create the ultimate photo album(s). inspired again by *oblation*.

covet:
oblation papers hand-crafted cards
tenshineko shopping bag
good indian girls do design! cards
yee haw industries cards
proletariat industries toilet paper covers
mudlark stationery collections
agatha ruiz de la prada pencil case

odessa

chic boutique

410 sw 13th avenue. between washington and burnside
503.223.1998
mon - sat 11a - 7p sun noon - 6p

opened in 1996. owner: susan tompkins
all major credit cards accepted

southwest : downtown > **s29**

back in the early days of the pearl district, there were not a lot of places to shop. but susan was a pioneer and opened *odessa*, and the ever-growing population of women in portland who knew the what's what with style, headed there. since then *odessa* moved to a different location in the pearl, but it wasn't the right fit. finally this last july, *odessa* settled into a sweet little spot in pdx's coolest two-block 'hood of which some are calling the west end. here susan can best show her fresh mix of mayle and daryl k and anna cohen. salutations to *odessa* for finding the perfect home.

covet:
mayle clothing & shoes
loomstate
daryl k
cacharel
anna cohen
kerry cassill linens & bedding
repetto shoes

office

quality products for the modern worker
2204 ne alberta street. corner of 22nd
888.355.SHOP (7467) www.officepdx.com
tue - fri 11a - 7p sat 11a - 5p sun noon - 4p

opened in 2005. owners: kelly coller and tony secolo
all major credit cards accepted
online shopping. events

northeast : alberta > s30

i feel like there's some sort of vulcan mind-meld happening with tony, kelly and me. if there's a product i really lust after, i can guarantee that when i walk into *office*, they will have it. how do they know this? before i can yap to them about my love of all things japanese, they tell me they're off to tokyo to source the coolest in that country's office sundries. either we're long-separated triplets (which would be scary because they are married) or wait, maybe we just like the same things!?! that's got to be it because there's nothing in *office* that i don't want in a big, bad way.

covet:
groovy japanese binders, paper goods &
   laptop bags
jack spade ping-pong paddle covers
blu dot desk accessories & furniture
russel & hazel and m.o. binders
faune yerby contact sheet decoupage
everything rhodia
acme made laptop bags

opal

ladies made-to-measure, collaborative clothing
1925 nw overton street suite 102. between 19th and 20th
503.445.4388 www.opalcollaborative.com
tue - sat 10a - 6:30p

opened in 2006. owner: meg okies
mc. visa
custom patterns. custom kits. fabric by the yard

northwest : nob hill > **s31**

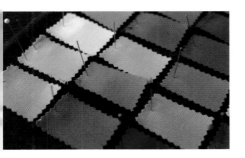

when i go overseas, i dream of getting clothing made that is custom fit for my figure. but now with the advent of *opal*, the dream becomes local. praise be to meg that she realized there was a need in the market for beautifully made, custom-fit wardrobe staples. here's how it works: you come in, pick your style and length (just skirts and pants are available at this time), have your measurements taken (while sipping a bit of champagne) and choose a fabric color (the fabric is a gorgeous super 120 italian merino wool). two weeks later you'll have a piece that will last you a lifetime. superb.

covet:
skirts:
   pencil
   a-line frontpleat
   princess with flare
   contoured
pants:
   short gaucho
   wide leg slack
   straight

phlox

women's clothing & accessories
3962 n mississippi. between shaver and failing
503.890.0715 www.phloxpdx.com
tue - sun 11a - 6p

opened in 2006. owner: barbara seipp
all major credit cards accepted

recently i was talking about how the *eat.shop guides* were not only about eating and shopping, but also about people making life transitions. often these changes can be a real struggle (who am i? what do i want to do with my life?), but sometimes a dream or vision is so strong, the transition loses some of its sting. barbara made this change—a lawyer by trade, she knew that designing clothing was her passion. too bad for the legal trade, but fantastic for the rest of us that she opened *phlox* where you can find her feminine designs and other beautiful pieces that will evolve your wardrobe.

covet:
clothing:
  barbara seipp
  tibi
  lewis cho
  corey lynn calter
giraudon shoes
modern vintage shoes
kim white hand bags

polliwog

groovy children's clothing

2900 se belmont street. corner of 29th
503.236.3903 www.polliwogportland.com
mon - sat 10a - 6p sun 11a - 5p

opened in 2005. owners: chris raak and phoebe smith buls
mc. visa
gift registry

southeat : belmont > **s33**

last fall, i went back-to-school shopping with my mom and lola. i took them to *polliwog* and i don't know who was more taken with the store. my mom was on one side of the store oohing and aahing over the swingy ponchos and jewel-toned chinese vests, while my daughter was on the other side calling out like a miniature drill seargent "come! beautiful! dresses!" it was a free-for-all, but at *polliwog* it's hard to stop yourself because everywhere you look there are fantastic t's or beautiful toys or … i could go on and on. just know that before you go, restraint of any form, will be difficult.

covet:
mr. tiny
imps & elfs
bobo brooklyn t's & capes
portland luv munster
rockin' baby slings
kumquat
kingsley t's
woody click modern dollhouses

portland modern

'40s - '70s mid-century modern
2109 nw irving (basement entrance on 21st). corner of 21st
503.243.2580
tue - sun 11:30a - 6p

opened in 2005. owner: heath webb
mc. visa

northwest : nob hill > s34

i can't count how often i drive down northwest 21st, but it's a lot. one day i noticed there was a store at the bottom of the building on the corner of irving. hmmm, what's this? after heading down into the basement, i was gob-smacked (sorry to use british slang, but i love this term) to find the two big rooms of *portland modern* teeming with great mid-century swag. "zowie!" i thought to myself, "this place must be brand new and i'm the super-discoverer." just turns out i'm blind, as *portland modern* has been open for over a year in this stealth location. so now i know and so do you.

covet:
burke tulip table & chair set
1964 quilted black vinyl bar
harlequin barrel sofa & chairs
swanky sideboards
welcome back cotter board game
mod fireplace
'70s hitachi tv's

possession

beautiful objects both antique and contemporary

1204 nw glisan. corner of 12th
503.224.9220 www.possessiononline.com
mon - sat 11a - 6p sun 11a - 5p

opened in 2005. owner: stephanie morrow
all major credit cards accepted
design consultation. custom furniture

northwest : pearl district > **s35**

i often feel like i could live in a completely modern house, surrounded by sleek, modern objects. but after i spend time in a place like *possession*, that all goes out the window because i'm reminded of the beautiful patina of vintage objects. stephanie has created a lush, romantic world at *possession* mixing antiques from britain and france and vintage glassware and pewter with charming modern-day jewelry and accessories. so now i'll be embracing a bit of the old and the new world in my home which feels like the perfect contemporary mix.

covet:
hand-crafted antiqued french-style
    upholstered furniture
british antiques
michael michaud jewelry, boxes & table art
angela vertopoulos ocean-inspired jewelry
gorgeous vintage bottles
1920s german fabric duvets
glass-beaded chandeliers

quinn in the city

flowers for weddings, events and everyday happiness
at city market: 735 nw 21st avenue. corner of johnson
503.752.6633
mon - sat 9:30a - 7p sun 10a - 7p

opened in 2005. owner: quinn kyle
all major credit cards accepted
custom orders. delivery

northwest : nob hill > **s36**

i will be completely up front with you. i have known quinn since high school and we have a deep bond that we rarely share with anybody: we were both trojanes. yes friends, i have pictures of quinn and myself wearing full-body electric-blue lycra jumpsuits. because i've just made this public knowledge, i will make amends to quinn and let you know that since then she has become a very talented florist. from the time she set up shop at *city market* a bit over a year ago, she has totally transformed the entrance into a lush garden of delights, and i swear her bouquets will make any day sunnier.

covet:
lush tropical flowers from hawaii
hand-tied european bouquets
custom hanging baskets &
   patio pots
loads of gorgeous cut flowers &
   potted plants
colorful and recyclable blume box vases
seasonal stems from local growers

shag

mid-century furniture and artifacts
4071 ne sandy boulevard. corner of 41st
503.493.7011 www.shagmidcentury.com
mon - fri 11a - 6p sat - sun 11a - 5p

opened in 2001. owners: cindy hislope and randy lucas
mc. visa

northeast : hollywood > s37

for years the hollywood district has been the rip van winkle of portland—sleeping away, but you know when it awakens, it will be bright and fresh. the sleepiness is wearing off with businesses like shag opening. one of the things i like most about this place is the big, exposed brick wall—who knew in hollywood there would be a space that felt a bit industrial and yet had everything from fat albert lunch boxes to a slammin' collection of '70s hi-fi equipment? now i know where to go to get a turntable to play my *sweet* and *pablo cruise* albums.

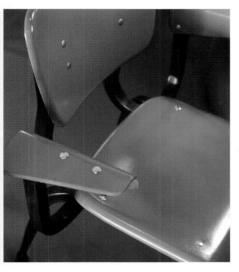

covet:
frem røjle chairs
welby clock
saarinen for knoll #71 series chairs
'70s desk chair
danish modern domino mobler desk
fat albert & the cosby kids lunch box
vintage hi-fi equipment

souchi

hand-loomed, hand-finished 100% cashmere
807 nw 23rd avenue. between johnson and kearney
503.525.0043 www.souchi.com/retail
daily 11a - 6p

opened in 2004. owner: suzi johnson
all major credit cards accepted
special orders

northwest : nob hill > s38

i'm a cashmere junky. but then i moved into a house that is the restaurant du jour for every cashmere-chomping moth in town. i swear they gather and say "which of kaie's cashmeres should we devour today? her black tunic is tasty, but the orange hoodie is to die for." but i won't let the little buggers win—because i must own a *souchi* plunge top and an oversize sweater for fall. and now that *souchi* has moved into a plush new space, i will be even more tempted. so moths, be warned, you're outta my house because *souchis* are coming in.

covet:
all souchi knits—especially the
   ribbed waist plunge top
souchi oversized sweaters for fall
jovovich-hawk clothing
lyell clothing
rachel mara clothing
hazel cox jewelry
thea grant jewelry

space design

a home and garden company

3729 sw kelly avenue. enter on lane
503.274.8800 www.spacedesignonline.com
by appointment only or first saturday of the month 10a - 4p

opened in 2005. owner: martie accuardi
mc. visa
custom floral design. botanical bar. planting parties
classes. interior microdesign. garden design

southwest : lair hill > **s39**

when i talk to orchids, this is what they say to me "shhh, you're making us wilt." when martie talks to orchids they say, "we'll do anything you ask." this is why martie is the orchid whisperer. and her talents don't stop there: garden, floral and interior design are just a few of her other specialities and you get the feeling that anything she touches blooms. to have a bit of martie's magic rub off on you, schedule a planting party at *space design* with a group of friends to create stunning orchid arrangements under martie's creative guidance. i think even the orchids would allow me to do this.

covet:
orchid of the month club (quarterly or yearly)
beautiful vases & containers
corals & ocean paraphernalia
thomas paul pillows
karim rashid umbra chairs
compelling artwork
io herbal alchemy potions & balms

switch shoes

shoes out of the box
7871 sw capitol highway. corner of 36th
503.445.4585 www.switch-shoes.com
mon - sat 10a - 6p sun 11a - 4p

opened in 2006. owners: rina menashe and jennifer robinson
mc. visa
online shopping

southwest : multnomah village > **s40**

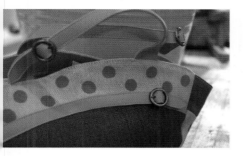

sometimes it's hard not to get consumed with day-to-day aggravations. but one of the ways that i shake myself out of a malaise is to wear something really outrageous, funky and bright. if you subscribe to this dressing theory, then truck on over to *switch shoes*. rina and jennifer carry the coolest, funkiest, most vibrantly-colored shoes around. from the exit line that rina discovered in israel to camper, the shoes are all ones that are destined to be noticed. in fact, i guarantee whatever you buy from *switch* will garner you the "wherrrreeee did you get those shoes" greeting.

covet:
shoes:
  exit
  camper
  fly london
  el naturalista
laura bee bags
morgen barrett jewelry
ayala bar jewelry

the lippman company

your party store
50 se yamhill street. corner of water
503.239.7007 www.lippmancompany.com
mon - fri 9a - 7p sat 9a - 6p

opened in 1948. owners: steve lippman and vicki french lippman
mc. visa
online shopping. custom balloon imprinting. rentals
party and event space (www.1050events.com)

southeast : industrial district >

though i've been off the party-giving circuit for the last couple of years, i did spend the majority of my 20s and 30s throwing casserole parties and "eew, ick, it's february" bashes. but here it is 2006 and i'm beginning to feel the party party party urge again. if you have the party itch too, *the lippman company* is the place to scratch it. not only do they have a vast, warehouse-sized space filled with everything from balloons to tiki's to disco balls, they also have a space next door (*studio ten-fifty*) to have your parties in. love these guys. they make it easy to partay all the time.

covet:
big colorful paper daisies
vast amounts of decorations for every holiday
bins & bins of goodie-bag goodies
tiki & luau necessities
balloons of all shapes & sizes
colorful small & large tissue balls
bottles of fake blood
small & large disco balls

una

eclectric, romantically edgy women's boutique
2802 se ankeny. corner of 28th
503.235.2326 www.una-myheartisfull.com
tue - sat 11a - 6p sun noon - 5p

opened in 2005. owner: giovanna parolari
mc. visa

southeast : 28th > s42

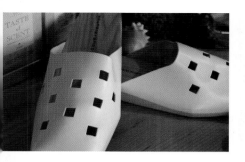

recently i've begun to clean out my closet. the moment i started to clear things out, i felt the need to just chuck it all and start over at *una*. and when i go for my closet refill, i'll need a couple of uninterrupted moments so i can visit each perfect garment, give it a greeting, and whisper to it that it really needs to come and live with me. either i'm not the only one to do this, or giovanna just knows that i'm a kook, so she gives me my space. regardless, the clothes at *una* are some of the most gorgeous to be found in portland or for that matter, anywhere.

covet:
tibi tunics & dresses
catherine andre knits
dévastee t's
vena cava dresses & tops
hengst dresses, tunics & pants
linea dresses & tops
thorn jewelry
alice park wallets

yes

it's the small things that make life rich
811 e burnside suite #116. between 8th and 9th
503.236.7788 www.yespdx.com
mon - sat 11a - 7p sun noon - 6p

opened in 2004. owner: charlotte lavictoire
mc. visa

northeast : burnside > s43

oui. si. ja. nguh mah. hai. doesn't matter, yes always means the same thing: okay. good. i'll take everything. oops, that last one pertains only to *yes*, the boutique. when charlotte moved her fresh boutique into its stunning new space late in 2005, cheers were heard all around portland. *yes* had a fan base before, but now its popularity has soared to new heights. and charlotte's not done with the transformation. because she loves the lifestyle concept, *yes* will focus more on intriguing, useful objects for the home and self. ano. ne. yippee!

covet:
mary meyer soft jersey pieces
amy tavern steel & gold jewelry
8020 footwear
lifetime for men
anzevino & florence for men & women
donna lou clothing
noted egglings
kari merkl lighting

etc.

the eat.shop guides were created by kaie wellman and are published by cabazon books
for more information about the series: www.eatshopguides.com

eat.shop.portland was written, researched and photographed by kaie wellman

copy editing: lynn king   fact checking: summer browner
map design and production: ligature laboratories - kieran lynn, jim anderson, erin cheek and kate emmons

kaie thx: each and every business in this book. the city of portland which is the coolest big town, litte city in the united states. my parents who give me incredible encouragement and support. my friends and family who are incredibly patient while i take pictures of their food when we go out to dinner together. to pat for all her help. and finally to kevin and lola, who are quite simply, the best.

cabazon books: eat.shop.portland 4th edition
ISBN 0-9747325-9-1

every effort has been made to ensure the accuracy of the information in this book. however, certain details are subject to change. please remember when using the guides that hours alter seasonally and some-times sadly, businesses close. the publisher cannot accept responsibility for any consequences arising from the use of this book.

the eat.shop guides are distributed by independent publishers group: www.ipgbook.com

PRINTED IN SINGAPORE